MW00526858

To

....

From

....

Date

....

3-MINUTE DEVOTIONS
for Hope and Healing

JOANNE SIMMONS

BARBOUR
PUBLISHING

Published by Barbour Publishing, Inc., 1810 Barbour Drive, Uhrichsville, Ohio 44683, www.barbourbooks.com

Our mission is to inspire the world with the life-changing message of the Bible.

Member of the
Evangelical Christian
Publishers Association

Printed in China.

Hope and Healing for Your Beautiful Heart

These devotions were written especially for those moments when you need a little reminder that your heavenly Creator offers all the hope and healing your heart needs—today and every day. Just three tiny minutes will help to comfort and encourage your spirit.

- Minute 1: Read the day's Bible verse and reflect on its meaning.

- Minute 2: Read the devotion and think about its application to your life.

- Minute 3: Pray.

Although these devotions aren't meant as a tool for deep Bible study, they can be a touch point to keep you grounded and focused on God, the One who listens to your every prayer. May every moment you spend with this book be a blessing!

The Things That Are Above

If then you have been raised with Christ, seek the
things that are above, where Christ is, seated at
the right hand of God. Set your minds on things
that are above, not on things that are on earth.
COLOSSIANS 3:1-2 ESV

If you believe in and have received Jesus Christ as your one and only Savior from your sin, then you have been raised with Christ, and you have every reason to celebrate! Our hope and healing are in Christ. Our real life is in Christ. If we focus on the things of earth, where everything will pass away, we have no hope, no healing. Instead, we must lift our minds to focus on those "things that are above" this temporary, broken world—where Christ is seated at the right hand of God in the perfect forever kingdom of heaven, and where all who have been raised with Christ truly belong.

Dear Jesus, please help me keep my mind set far
above this hopeless, hurting world. All of my life,
all of my hope and healing are in You alone. Amen.

Be Intentional

For you have died, and your life is hidden with
Christ in God. When Christ who is your life appears,
then you also will appear with him in glory.
Put to death therefore what is earthly in you.

COLOSSIANS 3:3–5 ESV

How exactly do we focus on the things above when we are planted here in this broken world? Countless trials, temptations, distractions, hardships, and wounds pull our minds away from God above—and His Word says we must put all those things to death! We have to be intentional and willing to work to keep our attention fixed where it should be, with a life devoted to learning from and living for God—through the study of His Word, through prayer, through devoted worship, through service to others, and through active participation in His Church for the fellowship we need with other believers. We must remember our life here on earth is temporary and ask God to show us His purposes and plans. We seek His guidance moment by moment and day by day, trusting that He is working all things together for good for those who love Him (Romans 8:28).

Heavenly Father, please help me put to death what
is earthly in me. Help me to be intentional, like
You are, every moment to keep my mind focused
above—on You and Your perfect plans. Amen.

Part of the Body

Now you are the body of Christ and individually
members of it. And God has appointed in the church
first apostles, second prophets, third teachers,
then miracles, then gifts of healing, helping,
administrating, and various kinds of tongues.

1 CORINTHIANS 12:27–28 ESV

You became part of the Body of Christ when you received
Jesus as your Savior. Everyone who is saved is part of the
Body. And to have real hope and healing throughout all of
your life, being an active part of a local fellowship of believers
is crucial. Are you involved in a healthy local church where
each member knows his or her unique gifts and uses them
in collaboration to care for each other and to further God's
kingdom? Read all of 1 Corinthians 12 and pray for God to
lead you if you have not found that kind of church yet. And
if you already have, pray regularly for God to protect and
develop your church and help it continue to thrive.

Heavenly Father, thank You that I am part of Your
body of believers. Please heal us, fill us continually
with hope in You, and keep us healthy. Amen.

All Who Touched Him Were Healed

The people recognized Jesus at once, and they ran throughout the whole area, carrying sick people on mats to wherever they heard he was. Wherever he went—in villages, cities, or the countryside—they brought the sick out to the marketplaces. They begged him to let the sick touch at least the fringe of his robe, and all who touched him were healed.

MARK 6:54-56 NLT

How heartbreaking it must have been to see so many sick people in the villages and towns and rural areas where Jesus went. But how amazing to see Jesus heal them with even just a touch to the fringe of His robe! Imagine the awe and relief and rejoicing and celebration! Our minds can barely comprehend it. Though we don't have Jesus in the flesh with us today so we can witness His miraculous healing firsthand, we do have the Holy Spirit He sent to us. The same power of God in the Holy Spirit is able to heal and do anything God chooses.

Dear Jesus, I wish I could have seen You in person here on earth, but I trust in Your healing power. I trust that Your Holy Spirit is here now and is able to heal and do absolutely anything according to God's will. I pray that Your will be done in all things. Amen.

Take Every Thought Captive

Though we live in the world, we do not wage war as the world does. The weapons we fight with are not the weapons of the world. On the contrary, they have divine power to demolish strongholds. We demolish arguments and every pretension that sets itself up against the knowledge of God, and we take captive every thought to make it obedient to Christ.

2 CORINTHIANS 10:3–5 NIV

Every trial, temptation, or distraction that hinders our hope and our healing can be demolished through the power of God working within us. Satan, our enemy, is always working in this world to spread his lies and destruction. But God is greater, and with His help, we can capture each and every thought and argument that opposes Him and make it obedient to Christ. What does this look like in your life? What thoughts and arguments that oppose God's truth pester and plague you the most? How are you capturing them and making them obedient to Christ?

Heavenly Father, please make me wise and discerning and powerful against the strongholds and lies of this world that the enemy uses to try to separate me from You. I want my every thought captivated by and focused on You! Amen.

Steadfast Savior

Jesus Christ is the same yesterday
and today and forever.

HEBREWS 13:8 NIV

Loss of a loved one can create devastating feelings of hope-lessness and despair and wounds so painful they feel like they will never fully heal. The changes in life resulting from the absence of that loved one are confusing and overwhelming. It's hard to know if anything will ever feel normal again; it's easy to feel anxious every moment, wondering who or what you might lose next. And so the truth that Jesus Christ is the same yesterday, today, and forever is your anchor—steady, strong, and sure. Yes, life is full of unpredictable loss in this broken world. But you can never lose your Savior or the assurance that He never changes and is preparing your heavenly home, where you'll live forever in perfect paradise.

Dear Jesus, be my steady anchor. Help me to
trust that no matter what is changing around me
or what loss or despair I'm suffering, You remain
the same. You are my steadfast Savior. Amen.

The Power of God for Salvation

For I am not ashamed of the gospel, for it is the power of God for salvation to everyone who believes.

ROMANS 1:16 ESV

When we suffer the loss of a loved one, we can rejoice even in the midst of our heartache if we know our loved one had received Jesus Christ as Savior. If we are not confident of that, we will experience deeper pain and sorrow. In either case, the loss can motivate us to share the gospel more boldly, more frequently, and more sincerely in hopes that more people will listen and repent and receive Christ as the one and only Way, Truth, and Life—and secure their heavenly home for the future.

Heavenly Father, please help me to use the pain of losing a loved one to motivate me to share Your message of salvation and eternal life with more and more people who desperately need to hear it. Amen.

The Birds Will Remind You

"Are not two sparrows sold for a penny? And not one of them will fall to the ground apart from your Father. But even the hairs of your head are all numbered. Fear not, therefore; you are of more value than many sparrows."
MATTHEW 10:29-31 ESV

Do you have favorite birds you like to watch or whose songs you love to hear? Every time you see or hear God's avian creatures, think of this scripture and let it remind you how much you are loved and valued by your heavenly Father. If God knows and cares about every single sparrow, He surely knows and cares about you—so much so that He sent His Son to die to save you. He knows you so well that He has even counted the hairs on your head. He is good and sovereign over your life. Place all your hope in Him—there's no better place it could be!

Heavenly Father, I can't even begin to understand how You know everything about everything and everything about me too. But I am so grateful for Your love and care and salvation through Jesus. Amen.

Healing in His Wings

*The LORD of Heaven's Armies says, "The day of
judgment is coming, burning like a furnace. On that
day the arrogant and the wicked will be burned up like
straw. They will be consumed—roots, branches, and all.
But for you who fear my name, the Sun of Righteousness
will rise with healing in his wings. And you will go
free, leaping with joy like calves let out to pasture."*

MALACHI 4:1-2 NLT

Sometimes we think we can't heal from emotional pain until
we get justice for wrongdoing against us. But we may never
actually see that justice delivered in this life; and whether
we do or not, we must heed the apostle Paul's words in the
book of Romans, where he admonishes, "Dear friends, never
take revenge. Leave that to the righteous anger of God. For
the Scriptures say, 'I will take revenge; I will pay them back,'
says the LORD" (Romans 12:19 NLT). God sees and knows any
wrongdoing against you. Let His righteous anger take care of
it. Trust His perfect justice, and believe that He will heal you.

*Heavenly Father, I need Your wisdom and self-control
when I think about how I want justice for wrongdoing
against me. I am trusting that You alone deliver
perfect justice. I give my anger and pain to You.
Please replace them with peace and healing. Amen.*

Act as True Children of God

"Love your enemies! Pray for those who persecute you! In that way, you will be acting as true children of your Father in heaven. For he gives his sunlight to both the evil and the good, and he sends rain on the just and the unjust alike. If you love only those who love you, what reward is there for that? Even corrupt tax collectors do that much. If you are kind only to your friends, how are you different from anyone else? Even pagans do that. But you are to be perfect, even as your Father in heaven is perfect."

MATTHEW 5:44-48 NLT

Whether we see justice for wrongdoing against us or not, God calls us to love our enemies and pray for those who persecute us. That instruction might seem absolutely upside-down crazy and impossible, but Jesus would not have taught it if it were not good for us. When we love our enemies and pray for those who persecute us, we draw closer to our heavenly Father as we become more like Him. And the closer we are to Him and the more we act like Him, the more we experience hope and healing.

Dear Jesus, through Your great power, please help me to do what seems impossible—help me to love my enemies and pray for those who persecute me. Amen.

The Greatness of His Love

Christ will make his home in your hearts as you trust in him. Your roots will grow down into God's love and keep you strong. And may you have the power to understand, as all God's people should, how wide, how long, how high, and how deep his love is. May you experience the love of Christ, though it is too great to understand fully. Then you will be made complete with all the fullness of life and power that comes from God. Now all glory to God, who is able, through his mighty power at work within us, to accomplish infinitely more than we might ask or think.

EPHESIANS 3:17-20 NLT

Sometimes we feel hopeless because we fail to realize and focus on God's amazing love for us. If we could fully understand the breadth and length and height and depth of His love, we would never worry or feel scared or hopeless about a thing ever again. Think on Jesus' sacrifice to save you from sin. Think on all the many other blessings in your life. Trust that God will continue to care for you. He is able to do so much more than you could ever dream.

Dear Jesus, help me to realize and focus on Your incredible love more and more each day. Amen.

No One Has to Crumble

"Why do you call me 'Lord, Lord,' and not do what I tell you? Everyone who comes to me and hears my words and does them, I will show you what he is like: he is like a man building a house, who dug deep and laid the foundation on the rock. And when a flood arose, the stream broke against that house and could not shake it, because it had been well built. But the one who hears and does not do them is like a man who built a house on the ground without a foundation. When the stream broke against it, immediately it fell, and the ruin of that house was great."

LUKE 6:46-49 ESV

Those who call Jesus Lord but don't actually do what He says are in danger of hopelessly caving and crumbling through life's hardship and pain. But no one has to live that way! Those who call Jesus Lord and actually listen and obey and have a relationship with Him—it's like they're building their lives on solid rock. When the rains and storms and floods of life come, those whose foundation is built on Jesus don't need to worry about crumbling and washing away. They will stand strong through anything because they stand on Jesus.

Dear Jesus, I want my life to be rock solid and strong because my foundation is obedience to You! Teach and build me through Your Holy Word. Amen.

The Tongues of the Wise Bring Healing

The words of the reckless pierce like swords,
but the tongue of the wise brings healing.

PROVERBS 12:18 NIV

When you find yourself suffering from an emotional wound, to whom do you go for a listening ear, to talk out the pain and seek help and healing? It's easy to want to vent to anyone who will listen, but be careful. Scripture is clear you should not go to those who are reckless with their words, for they might only pierce your wound and injure you more. Instead, be intentional to seek out people who are wise, because their tongues will bring healing. Do you have those wise people in your life? If not, pray for God's direction toward and connection with wise people who love Him and His Word, who will give you both compassion and good counsel in any hard situation.

Heavenly Father, help me to be careful whom I vent to when I am emotionally wounded and hurting. Please guide me to wise people who can truly help me to heal. Amen.

Words like Honey

*The heart of the wise has power over his mouth and
adds learning to his lips. Pleasing words are like honey.
They are sweet to the soul and healing to the bones.*

PROVERBS 16:23–24 NLV

What you say and what others say to you will make a difference in your ability to heal from emotional wounds. If you only
think and speak and hear negativity and bitterness, you will
wallow endlessly in negativity and bitterness. You absolutely
need the right times and places to let loose the reality of
your pain in healthy ways, but with God's help and wisdom,
you can maintain good self-control and keep learning and
growing through your situation. Seek out words from others
and seek to use words yourself that are pleasing like honey,
that bring sweetness to your soul and healing to your bones.

*Heavenly Father, help me to remove the thoughts and
words from my mind and lips that make me wallow in
pain. Fill me up with pleasing words to think and speak.
Focus my attention on Your goodness and love to me,
and please heal my wounds and heartache. Amen.*

He Took Jesus at His Word

*Once more he visited Cana in Galilee, where he had
turned the water into wine. And there was a certain
royal official whose son lay sick at Capernaum. When
this man heard that Jesus had arrived in Galilee
from Judea, he went to him and begged him to
come and heal his son, who was close to death.*

JOHN 4:46–47 NIV

The desperation and fear in this dad are hard to understand
unless one has been in his shoes, having lost or nearly lost a
child. He was a royal official but not too important or prideful
to beg Jesus for help. And when Jesus said only the words,
"Go, your son will live," the royal official stopped begging
for Jesus to come to his son. He "took Jesus at his word and
departed" (John 4:50 NIV). We too can take Jesus at His
Word, sight unseen. Those of us who trust in Him as Savior
are promised healing and eternal life. Sometimes miracles
of healing are God's will in this earthly life; ultimately, they
are His will for believers forevermore in heaven.

*Dear Jesus, even while desperate for the healing of
his son, the royal official took You at Your word and
trusted You completely—believed You had done the
healing—even before he saw the proof with his own
eyes. I want to have such great faith too. Amen.*

Truly Trustworthy

God is not man, that he should lie, or a son of man, that he should change his mind. Has he said, and will he not do it? Or has he spoken, and will he not fulfill it?

NUMBERS 23:19 ESV

If you have been lied to, let down, and betrayed too many times, you may have little to no hope of ever fully trusting any person again. When that fear of trusting threatens to send you spiraling into despair, instead let it urge you to cling harder to the One always worthy of every bit of your trust. He "has given both his promise and his oath. These two things are unchangeable because it is impossible for God to lie. Therefore, we who have fled to him for refuge can have great confidence as we hold to the hope that lies before us. This hope is a strong and trustworthy anchor for our souls" (Hebrews 6:18–19 NLT).

Heavenly Father, please heal my wounds from when I've been lied to, let down, and betrayed. Help me to cling to You most of all as my one true God, worthy of all my trust. And please lead me to the people who are filled with Your Spirit, who will befriend and love me in good and honest ways. Amen.

Don't Be Dismayed

"So do not fear, for I am with you; do not be dismayed,
for I am your God. I will strengthen you and help you;
I will uphold you with my righteous right hand."

ISAIAH 41:10 NIV

No matter what you are going through, you have hope in any and every situation because God is your God. He never leaves you. Think of a time in your past when you were positive you would not survive the pain or hardship. How did you make it through? God never left you. What ways and what people did He provide to rescue you? He was continually strengthening and helping you, always holding you up with His righteous right hand. When you remember and thank Him and praise Him for specific ways He has helped you in the past, you gain confident hope and trust that He will do so again—right now and in the future.

Heavenly Father, You alone are my God. You
have never left me, and You never will. In the past,
present, and future, I trust that You strengthen
and help me and hold me up. Amen.

Connection, Comfort, and Care

*Ruth replied, "Don't urge me to leave you or to turn
back from you. Where you go I will go, and where you
stay I will stay. Your people will be my people and
your God my God. Where you die I will die, and there
I will be buried. May the LORD deal with me, be it ever
so severely, if even death separates you and me."*

RUTH 1:16-17 NIV

To heal from the pain and grief caused by the loss of a loved
one, we need to connect and cling to other good and loving
relationships. Ruth's loyalty to Naomi after they had both
suffered loss is a beautiful example of how God healed and
blessed them both, as they depended on each other and
ultimately on God in the midst of their grief and great need.
Our enemy, Satan, wants to isolate us when we are in pain
so that he can wound us even more and try to completely
destroy us. So we must be intentional to connect with others
and let God's healing and protection and blessing flow to us
through the comfort and care of those loving people He has
placed in our lives.

*Heavenly Father, show me Your great love and healing
through the people You have placed in my life. Help me
to connect well with others, so I can receive the comfort
and care You want to give me through them. Amen.*

Commit Your Way to Him

Commit your way to the LORD; trust in him and he will do this: He will make your righteous reward shine like the dawn, your vindication like the noonday sun. Be still before the LORD and wait patiently for him; do not fret when people succeed in their ways, when they carry out their wicked schemes. Refrain from anger and turn from wrath; do not fret—it leads only to evil. For those who are evil will be destroyed, but those who hope in the LORD will inherit the land.

PSALM 37:5–9 NIV

In a difficult or unfair situation at work or in a relationship, you may feel hopeless. But take heart and wait patiently for God to act on your behalf. He sees and knows all the details. Commit your way to Him with obedience to Him and His Word. Constantly pray for wisdom and direction. Keep your faith, stay patient, and maintain your integrity as you trust in Him. And in His perfect timing, He will vindicate and reward you.

Lord, I'm struggling in this situation, but I know You will work on my behalf. I commit my way to You as I wait for Your perfect timing and Your perfect justice. Amen.

Don't Let Your Hands Lose Strength

The King of Israel, the Lord, is with you. You will not be afraid of trouble any more. On that day it will be said to Jerusalem: "Do not be afraid, O Zion. Do not let your hands lose their strength. The Lord your God is with you, a Powerful One Who wins the battle. He will have much joy over you. With His love He will give you new life. He will have joy over you with loud singing."

ZEPHANIAH 3:15-17 NLV

These words through the prophet Zephaniah to the people of Israel are written down in God's Word to help give you hope and healing today too. Keep a strong grip on God's hand that is gripping yours. If you feel yourself start to weaken, focus on the truth of how great God is in you, and hold on tight. Nothing compares to Him! No one can defeat Him! He will win this battle you are going through, just *do not let go* of your faith in Him. All your power and purpose are in Him. Soon you will be rejoicing together on the winning side of this hardship and pain.

Heavenly Father, thank You for Your strong grip on my life because I believe in You and have been saved by Your Son. You are my power and purpose. Help me always hold tightly to You! Amen.

We Are from God

We know that everyone who has been born of God does not keep on sinning, but he who was born of God protects him, and the evil one does not touch him. We know that we are from God, and the whole world lies in the power of the evil one. And we know that the Son of God has come and has given us understanding, so that we may know him who is true; and we are in him who is true, in his Son Jesus Christ. He is the true God and eternal life.

1 JOHN 5:18-20 ESV

The evil and sin in this world can feel overwhelming at times. Just trying to follow the news can cause fear and anxiety and depression. But God's Word gives us hope and peace and courage. Yes, the whole world is under the power of the evil one for now—but not forever. And while we wait for Jesus' return to make all things right and new, He protects us and promises us eternal life. We must never forget that we are from God, and greater is He who is in us than he who is in the world (1 John 4:4).

Heavenly Father, please help me not to become overwhelmed and discouraged by the evil and sin in the world. You are always greater in me than the evil one in the world. Amen.

Even with Unanswered Questions

That evening they brought to him many who were oppressed by demons, and he cast out the spirits with a word and healed all who were sick. This was to fulfill what was spoken by the prophet Isaiah: "He took our illnesses and bore our diseases."

MATTHEW 8:16–17 ESV

At times, reading the accounts of Jesus' healings might feel discouraging. You believe in the healing power of God and might wonder why He hasn't answered your prayers for healing for yourself or a loved one. Keep crying out to God with those questions. Let your pain and sorrow draw You closer to Him and never drive you away. Ask Him for supernatural comfort and peace and strength despite your questions and struggles. His healing is not always what we hope for and expect, but the promise is true that "He heals the brokenhearted and binds up their wounds" (Psalm 147:3 ESV).

Heavenly Father, even when I don't get answers to all of my questions, I choose to keep trusting in You. Pull me back to You if I ever start to turn away. Even in my pain and sorrow and confusion, I believe You are good and loving and sovereign. In You alone there is victory over sickness and death, and You will make all things new one day soon. Amen.

Hope in the Midst of Danger

Esther sent this reply to Mordecai: "Go and gather together all the Jews of Susa and fast for me. Do not eat or drink for three days, night or day. My maids and I will do the same. And then, though it is against the law, I will go in to see the king. If I must die, I must die."
ESTHER 4:15-16 NLT

Esther could have been killed for her boldness in speaking up to the king in defense of her people. But she hoped and trusted in the one true God. And because of her courage, her people, the Jews, were saved from the destruction intended by Haman's evil plans. Take time soon to read the whole book of Esther, and then anytime you need some extra faith and hope and courage, ask God to remind you of Esther's story and how He worked out His good plans to protect His people through her.

Heavenly Father, I want to have the courage of Esther in any hard or dangerous situation I face. Fill me up with trust in Your power and perfect plans. Amen.

In All Our Troubles

Praise be to the God and Father of our Lord Jesus
Christ, the Father of compassion and the God of
all comfort, who comforts us in all our troubles, so
that we can comfort those in any trouble with the
comfort we ourselves receive from God. For just
as we share abundantly in the sufferings of Christ,
so also our comfort abounds through Christ.

2 CORINTHIANS 1:3-5 NIV

In all our troubles, we will be comforted. God's Word promises that. And in all our troubles there is purpose, even when they seem so senseless. Whatever hardship or pain we go through, we receive abundant comfort from God that fills us up to overflowing so that we can pour it out onto others who need comfort. We must never turn away from God in times of trouble. Rather, we must draw even closer to Him, share in the sufferings of Christ, and lay hold of the camaraderie and compassion we find there so that we are full and ready to care well for others as God leads us.

Heavenly Father, I praise You for the compassion
and comfort You show me in every trial and
heartache. Fill me up to overflowing, and help me
share Your comfort with others so they too can
know Your great love and salvation. Amen.

Hope for a Hopeless Widow

*Then the word of the LORD came to [Elijah]: "Go at once
to Zarephath in the region of Sidon and stay there.
I have directed a widow there to supply you with food."*

1 KINGS 17:8-9 NIV

When the prophet Elijah found the widow, she told him
she didn't have any bread—just a little bit of flour and oil.
She was certain that she was about to make the very last
tiny meal for her son and herself and that they would soon
starve to death. Maybe you also have experienced that kind
of desperate resignation, either physically or spiritually or
both. But with God, you always have hope. He can provide
and rescue, just as He did through Elijah for the widow of
Zarephath. She obeyed the instruction from God through
His prophet and chose to trust that He would continue to
provide for her and her son, even while she provided for
Elijah first. And later on, she was rewarded far more greatly
when, after her son tragically died, Elijah brought him back
to life through God's miracle-working power.

*Heavenly Father, when I feel desperate with no
hope, remind me of Elijah and the widow. I pray that
You will provide and heal and rescue in miraculous
ways. I believe You can and will! Amen.*

Let the Tears Fall

You keep track of all my sorrows. You have collected all my tears in your bottle. You have recorded each one in your book.

PSALM 56:8 NLT

Not even our most devoted loved ones can possibly care for us as much as our heavenly Father does. Only He can literally keep track of every single tear we cry. Whatever pain and problems you are going through, take time to let yourself release the emotions. Don't hold them in, and don't think they don't matter to anyone. Let the tears fall freely—and instead of bottling them up inside yourself, let God be the One to bottle them up and comfort you in the midst of the sorrow. Trust His Word that "those who plant in tears will harvest with shouts of joy" (Psalm 126:5 NLT).

Heavenly Father, remind me—as I let the tears fall—that they never fall in vain. You keep track of my tears because You care about me that much, and You are healing me and giving me hope even in the midst of them. Amen.

Family Matters

Those who won't care for their relatives, especially those in their own household, have denied the true faith. Such people are worse than unbelievers.

1 TIMOTHY 5:8 NLT

Family matters to God. He has placed you in the family you have, and He expects you and your loved ones to take care of each other. He also knows that family relationships can be strained and broken and in desperate need of healing. If all parties involved humbly ask for and use God's help and wisdom, they can do their best to work things out with forgiveness and grace and love for each other. All families need to apply this scripture liberally: "Put on then, as God's chosen ones, holy and beloved, compassionate hearts, kindness, humility, meekness, and patience, bearing with one another and, if one has a complaint against another, forgiving each other; as the Lord has forgiven you, so you also must forgive. And above all these put on love, which binds everything together in perfect harmony" (Colossians 3:12–14 ESV).

Heavenly Father, thank You for my family. Please help us to love each other and take care of each other the way You want us to. Amen.

Through Everything God Has Made

*Ever since the world was created, people have seen the
earth and sky. Through everything God made, they can
clearly see his invisible qualities—his eternal power and
divine nature. So they have no excuse for not knowing God.*

ROMANS 1:20 NLT

At times we might feel hopeless, wondering if we are doing
enough to help people learn about God and have a chance
to be saved. But God promises in His Word that He has
shown Himself through everything He has made in creation.
Therefore, no one can say they know nothing about God.
Everyone can see Him in the tiny details of a pretty flower
and in the highest peaks of a rocky mountain range. He can
be seen in everything from the incredible design of our human
bodies to the ingenuity that animals show in building
homes for themselves. Our Creator God is awesome and
worthy of all our praise!

*Heavenly Father, thank You for making Yourself
known. I pray that more people will want to
grow closer to You through Jesus as a result
of seeing Your goodness in creation. Amen.*

Take Heart, Daughter

*Just then a woman who had been subject to bleeding
for twelve years came up behind him and touched the
edge of his cloak. She said to herself, "If I only touch
his cloak, I will be healed." Jesus turned and saw her.
"Take heart, daughter," he said, "your faith has healed
you." And the woman was healed at that moment.*

MATTHEW 9:20–22 NIV

If you've ever had a sickness that dragged on and on, you
know how sick of being sick you get—even for a matter of days
or weeks. The poor, bleeding woman in the Bible had been
sick for twelve *years!* But she had heard of Jesus, and she
had great faith in His power. She was sure that if she could
just touch the edge of His cloak, she would be healed. So
she did, and she was! Jesus is saying the same words to you
today—whatever you're going through: "Take heart, daughter.
Your faith has healed you." Even if not at this moment or even
in this life, Jesus will heal you forever in heaven.

*Dear Jesus, I take heart, and I have hope in You
alone. You have all power to heal and to give eternal
life. I praise You for this awesome truth! Amen.*

His Angels Will Hold You Up

*He will order his angels to protect you wherever
you go. They will hold you up with their hands
so you won't even hurt your foot on a stone.*

PSALM 91:11–12 NLT

The stories we hear about people experiencing angels sometimes seem like far-fetched fiction; but no matter the way some stories might be embellished, the Bible says angels are real. God helps us and protects us through their watch and care over our lives. Psalm 103:20–21 NLT says, "Praise the LORD, you angels, you mighty ones who carry out his plans, listening for each of his commands. Yes, praise the LORD, you armies of angels who serve him and do his will!"

*Heavenly Father, thank You for Your mighty
angels who obey Your commands and who watch
over me. I feel secure and loved and hopeful
because of Your care and protection. Amen.*

Remember Anna

*Anna, a prophet, was also there in the Temple. She was
the daughter of Phanuel from the tribe of Asher, and she
was very old. Her husband died when they had been
married only seven years. Then she lived as a widow
to the age of eighty-four. She never left the Temple but
stayed there day and night, worshiping God with fasting
and prayer. She came along just as Simeon was talking
with Mary and Joseph, and she began praising God.
She talked about the child to everyone who had been
waiting expectantly for God to rescue Jerusalem.*
LUKE 2:36-38 NLT

Anna lost her husband after only a short marriage and surely
must have suffered with grief. But she found hope and healing
through total devotion to God with day-and-night worship
through fasting and prayer. What a blessing that she was
able to see the infant Jesus, the long-awaited Messiah, with
her own eyes!

*Heavenly Father, when I suffer loss, remind me
through Anna's example that great hope and
healing can be found through spending my time
devoted to You in worship, fasting, and prayer.
Please bless me as You blessed Anna. Amen.*

Help from the Maker of Heaven and Earth

I lift up my eyes to the mountains—where does my help come from? My help comes from the LORD, the Maker of heaven and earth. He will not let your foot slip—he who watches over you will not slumber; indeed, he who watches over Israel will neither slumber nor sleep. The LORD watches over you—the LORD is your shade at your right hand; the sun will not harm you by day, nor the moon by night. The LORD will keep you from all harm—he will watch over your life.

PSALM 121:1-7 NIV

When you feel hopeless, look up! Remember where your help comes from—from the Maker of heaven and earth! Fix your thoughts on His greatness and His devoted care of you. Worship and praise Him! He never tires or falters in watching over you. You can rest well, because He never takes a rest. He will keep you from all harm.

Dear Lord, I look up to You for my help and hope. And at night I lie down in peace, knowing You never stop watching over me. Thank You! Amen.

Total Transformation

Meanwhile, Saul was uttering threats with every breath and was eager to kill the Lord's followers. So he went to the high priest. He requested letters addressed to the synagogues in Damascus, asking for their cooperation in the arrest of any followers of the Way he found there. He wanted to bring them—both men and women—back to Jerusalem in chains. As he was approaching Damascus on this mission, a light from heaven suddenly shone down around him. He fell to the ground and heard a voice saying to him, "Saul! Saul! Why are you persecuting me?" "Who are you, lord?" Saul asked. And the voice replied, "I am Jesus, the one you are persecuting! Now get up and go into the city, and you will be told what you must do."

ACTS 9:1-6 NLT

No matter the sin people get themselves involved in—even the persecution and murder of innocent people—hope can be found in Jesus Christ. The story of Saul, later called Paul, is a prime example of this truth. Jesus called him out of his evil life and completely turned his life around. And Jesus is still in the business of doing total transformations today.

Dear Jesus, I have great faith in Your power to totally transform any person and call them out of any kind of sinful lifestyle. I praise You for Your awesome work as the one true Savior! Amen.

Hope in the Simple Things

*"Go out and stand before me on the mountain," the LORD
told him. And as Elijah stood there, the LORD passed by,
and a mighty windstorm hit the mountain. It was such
a terrible blast that the rocks were torn loose, but the
LORD was not in the wind. After the wind there was an
earthquake, but the LORD was not in the earthquake. And
after the earthquake there was a fire, but the LORD was
not in the fire. And after the fire there was the sound of a
gentle whisper. When Elijah heard it, he wrapped his face
in his cloak and went out and stood at the entrance of the
cave. And a voice said, "What are you doing here, Elijah?"*

1 KINGS 19:11–13 NLT

Sometimes when we're expecting or hoping for God to speak
to us or act in an amazing and mighty way, He chooses to
surprise us in a simple way instead—like in this story from
1 Kings, where God let Elijah experience a powerful wind
and earthquake and fire. But God chose to reveal Himself to
Elijah through the sound of a gentle whisper. Have hope, and
be listening for God in even the simplest things in your life.

*Heavenly Father, help me to notice how You
are bringing me hope and healing in even the
simplest, most unassuming ways. Amen.*

Let God Refresh You

*If you pour yourself out for the hungry and satisfy
the desire of the afflicted, then shall your light rise
in the darkness and your gloom be as the noonday.
And the LORD will guide you continually and satisfy
your desire in scorched places and make your bones
strong; and you shall be like a watered garden,
like a spring of water, whose waters do not fail.*

ISAIAH 58:10–11 ESV

Like a near-death plant we keep forgetting to water, sometimes we start to feel dry and ugly in our souls when we aren't
spending good time with God. We need to read His Word
and pray and worship Him so that He can lead and refresh
us. He can give the kind of living water that enables us to
never feel thirsty or dry again! In this passage He says we
are satisfied and refreshed when we are pouring ourselves
out to help others in need. God is so good to continually fill
us up so that we always have plenty to share.

*Heavenly Father, please help me pour out my life
in service and care of others in exactly the ways
You want me to. As I do, thank You for refreshing
me with Your extraordinary living water! Amen.*

Water That Wells Up to Eternal Life

Jesus, wearied as he was from his journey,
was sitting beside the well.... A woman
from Samaria came to draw water.

JOHN 4:6-7 ESV

Jesus said to the Samaritan woman at the well, "If you knew
the gift of God, and who it is that is saying to you, 'Give me
a drink,' you would have asked him, and he would have
given you living water" (John 4:10 ESV). The woman didn't
understand. She said to Jesus, "You have nothing to draw
water with, and the well is deep. Where do you get that
living water?" (verse 11 ESV). Jesus told her, "Everyone who
drinks of this water will be thirsty again, but whoever drinks
of the water that I will give him will never be thirsty again.
The water that I will give him will become in him a spring
of water welling up to eternal life" (verses 13-14 ESV). So the
woman said, "Sir, give me this water" (verse 15 ESV).

Dear Jesus, please help me to be like the woman
at the well. She trusted that You give the kind
of water that makes people never thirst again
and leads to eternal life. I trust and hope in You
too—please quench and refresh me! Amen.

Hope Comes from God

*Our hope comes from God. May He fill you with joy
and peace because of your trust in Him. May your
hope grow stronger by the power of the Holy Spirit.*
ROMANS 15:13 NLV

Think about the things you hope for. Do you have a long list?
How have you seen your hopes change with life and experience and maturity? The reason we have any hope for good
things at all is because God is the giver of hope. Every good
and perfect gift comes from Him, James 1:17 tells us. And our
ultimate, final hope is in the promise of heaven, where there
will be no more sickness, sadness, or pain—only perfect
paradise forever as God dwells with us. With each new day,
let your hope in God and His good gifts grow stronger and
stronger by the power of the Holy Spirit in you.

*Heavenly Father, thank You for giving me
hope. All gifts and good things come from
You, and I trust that You have good plans
for me here on earth and a perfect forever
waiting for me in heaven with You. Amen.*

The Healing of the Centurion's Servant

When he had entered Capernaum, a centurion came forward to him, appealing to him, "Lord, my servant is lying paralyzed at home, suffering terribly." And he said to him, "I will come and heal him." But the centurion replied, "Lord, I am not worthy to have you come under my roof, but only say the word, and my servant will be healed. For I too am a man under authority, with soldiers under me. And I say to one, 'Go,' and he goes, and to another, 'Come,' and he comes, and to my servant, 'Do this,' and he does it." When Jesus heard this, he marveled and said to those who followed him, "Truly, I tell you, with no one in Israel have I found such faith."

MATTHEW 8:5-10 ESV

This army captain had such great faith in Jesus, he didn't even ask Jesus to come back to his house to heal his servant. He was humble, and he trusted Jesus could just say the word from anywhere and his servant would be healed. And the captain was absolutely right! Jesus said to him, " 'Go; let it be done for you as you have believed.' And the servant was healed at that very moment" (Matthew 8:13 ESV).

Heavenly Father, I want to have faith like this army captain. Help me to trust that You can simply say the word, and absolutely anything can happen! Amen.

Hope in the Midst of Trial

Don't be surprised at the fiery trials you are going through,
as if something strange were happening to you. Instead, be
very glad—for these trials make you partners with Christ
in his suffering, so that you will have the wonderful joy
of seeing his glory when it is revealed to all the world.

1 PETER 4:12-13 NLT

You can have hope in the midst of hardship when you re-member that your trials don't take God by surprise—and as hard as they are, your trials don't need to take you by sur-prise either. Jesus said, "Here on earth you will have many trials and sorrows. But take heart, because I have overcome the world" (John 16:33 NLT). God is sovereign over your current trial. He can rescue you at any moment, and He will in His perfect timing. Until then, trust that He sustains you and comforts you; He never leaves you. Scripture says you become partners with Him in His suffering as you endure your trial. Let Him use the time of suffering to bond you ever stronger and closer to Him—and one day you will share in the wonderful joy of seeing His glory revealed to all the world.

Dear Jesus, please draw me closer to You in the midst
of this trial. Help me to endure and learn and grow in
the ways You want me to. I trust You are sovereign and
good, and none of this takes You by surprise. Amen.

True Equality

For in Christ Jesus you are all sons of God, through faith. For as many of you as were baptized into Christ have put on Christ. There is neither Jew nor Greek, there is neither slave nor free, there is no male and female, for you are all one in Christ Jesus.

GALATIANS 3:26-28 ESV

Is there any hope for equality in our world? Yes—and Jesus alone offers true equality. Because of sin in the world, people will never get equality exactly right. There will always be evil ideologies spreading the lie that certain groups of people are better than others. But in God's eyes, because of Jesus, every single person is the same in value. We are all so loved by God that He sent Jesus to die to save us from our sins. And when we humbles ourselves, repent of sin, and trust in Jesus, we become children of the one true God, the King of all kings. That makes us all equally royal!

Heavenly Father, thank You that anyone can be Your child by trusting that only Jesus saves. You offer the only true equality through Him. Help me to share with others the awesome truth that we all have equal standing with You. Amen.

According to Your Faith

As Jesus went on from there, two blind men followed him, calling out, "Have mercy on us, Son of David!" When he had gone indoors, the blind men came to him, and he asked them, "Do you believe that I am able to do this?" "Yes, Lord," they replied. Then he touched their eyes and said, "According to your faith let it be done to you"; and their sight was restored.

MATTHEW 9:27-30 NIV

When you ask God for something in prayer, think of this passage of scripture where Jesus healed two blind men, restoring their sight. Tell Jesus what you need and then picture Him asking you, "Do you believe that I am able to do this?" Answer Him—yes, *Lord!*—and mean it. Tell Him you know without a doubt that He is able to do it. Then trust Him to answer your prayer according to His perfect will, His perfect timing, and His perfect plans.

Dear Jesus, I have hope and faith that You can do anything! Nothing I ask of You is ever too hard for You! Let Your will be done. I praise You! Amen.

The Lord—Your Strength and Rock

*I love you, O LORD, my strength. The LORD is my rock
and my fortress and my deliverer, my God, my rock,
in whom I take refuge, my shield, and the horn of my
salvation, my stronghold. I call upon the LORD, who is
worthy to be praised, and I am saved from my enemies.*

PSALM 18:1-3 ESV

Anytime something in your life feels shaky—maybe your
family or relationships are going through trouble, or you're
suffering from a job loss, or health problems are scaring you
or a loved one—remember that the Lord is your rock-solid
source of strength and stability. He promises that you will not
be shaken. Yes, things in your life might tremble and quake
at times; but ultimately, no matter what happens, God keeps
you safe and secure.

*Heavenly Father, You are strong and steady all the time—
in every place I am and in every problem I experience.
When things feel shaky in my life, please remind me to
keep my feet planted firmly on You, my solid rock. Amen.*

Learn from the Prodigal Son

"He arose and came to his father. But while he was still a long way off, his father saw him and felt compassion, and ran and embraced him and kissed him. And the son said to him, 'Father, I have sinned against heaven and before you. I am no longer worthy to be called your son.' But the father said to his servants, 'Bring quickly the best robe, and put it on him, and put a ring on his hand, and shoes on his feet. And bring the fattened calf and kill it, and let us eat and celebrate. For this my son was dead, and is alive again; he was lost, and is found.' And they began to celebrate."

LUKE 15:20-24 ESV

If you ever feel like you've messed up so much that you might never be forgiven—like you need to run away from a relationship or situation and never, ever come back—then think of the story Jesus told of the foolish son to help you remember that God loves you dearly *no matter what*. Just as the father in the story welcomed back his son who had made bad choices—with extravagant love and even a huge celebration—God, your heavenly Father, will welcome you back when you turn away from your sin and run into His open arms.

Heavenly Father, I can't thank You enough for Your endless love for me. In Your mercy, please lead me out of sinful patterns and mistakes and into Your truth and wisdom. Amen.

The Lord Lights the Darkness

You make my lamp bright.
The Lord my God lights my darkness.
PSALM 18:28 NLV

The darkness of hopelessness can be frighteningly deep—but it is never so deep that God cannot shine His light into it. In fact, the deeper the darkness, the brighter God's light in contrast. The darkness can never overcome it. If you find yourself wandering in darkness, with only more darkness in your view ahead, have you turned away from God's light? Sometimes circumstances that are no fault of our own drop us into the darkness of hopelessness, and sometimes our own willful choosing lands us there. But God's light never stops shining to guide us. We have to look for it and follow it. How? God can reveal His light in any way He chooses. Often He does so through our regular time in the truth of His Word, through moments of worship and prayer, and through fellowship with other believers.

Heavenly Father, when I find myself in darkness,
please light it up as only You can. I always
want to look for and follow You! Amen.

God Will Guide

*By day the LORD went ahead of them in a
pillar of cloud to guide them on their way and
by night in a pillar of fire to give them light, so
that they could travel by day or night. Neither
the pillar of cloud by day nor the pillar of fire
by night left its place in front of the people.*

EXODUS 13:21–22 NIV

Sometimes we hope and pray for God to guide us with the
same kind of impossible-to-miss signs in the sky that he gave
the Israelites in the wilderness. But even if His guidance is
not quite so clear and obvious, He will lead us just the same
when we are devoted to Him. His Word promises it: "Trust
in the LORD with all your heart and lean not on your own
understanding; in all your ways submit to him, and he will
make your paths straight" (Proverbs 3:5–6 NIV).

*Dear Lord, please lead and guide me and
make my paths straight. Help me to notice the
signs and directions You are giving me. I trust
You, and I submit my ways to You. Amen.*

The One Who Lifts Your Head

*Many are saying of me, "There is no help for him in
God." But You, O Lord, are a covering around me,
my shining-greatness, and the One Who lifts my head.
I was crying to the Lord with my voice. And He answered
me from His holy mountain. I lay down and slept,
and I woke up again, for the Lord keeps me safe.*

PSALM 3:2–5 NLV

Sometimes life feels so painful or depressing or frustrating
or scary or lonely that you just need to go to bed and cry
your eyes out. And that's okay! As you do, think of God
comforting you, envisioning Him, like this scripture says, as
the covering around you. He is the One who helps you and
gives you "shining-greatness" again. He lifts your head and
wants to help you get out of bed and face the hard things
going on. Crying out to God, pouring out all your feelings to
Him, can be incredibly beneficial; but then remember to let
Him lovingly lift your head and help you!

*Heavenly Father, I'm so grateful You let me cry
everything out to You. And then You lift my head
again with loving care. I can face anything with You
as my constant source of help and hope. Amen.*

Let Trouble Build Your Hope

We are glad for our troubles also. We know that troubles help us learn not to give up. When we have learned not to give up, it shows we have stood the test. When we have stood the test, it gives us hope. Hope never makes us ashamed because the love of God has come into our hearts through the Holy Spirit Who was given to us.

ROMANS 5:3–5 NLV

We never need to go asking for trouble; somehow it manages to find us all on its own. What trouble has come your way lately? Can you let Romans 5 help you think about it in a healthy, positive way? We can be glad about trouble by remembering that it helps us learn not to give up and strengthens our hope that things will be better in the future. When our hope is in the right place—in the almighty God, who has saved us through His Son and given us His Holy Spirit now and perfect life in heaven in the future—we will never be ashamed or defeated. Just as God sent His Son to save us at exactly the right time, He will deliver us out of any trouble at exactly the right time.

Heavenly Father, help me not to run away from trouble, but rather face it with Your power in me. You use trouble in my life to help me learn not to give up and to depend on You. You have saved me through Your Son, and You are my ultimate hope and peace. Amen.

Humble and Willing to Listen

*Now Naaman was commander of the army of the king of
Aram. He was a great man in the sight of his master and
highly regarded.... He was a valiant soldier, but he had
leprosy. Now bands of raiders from Aram had gone out and
had taken captive a young girl from Israel, and she served
Naaman's wife. She said to her mistress, "If only my master
would see the prophet who is in Samaria! He would cure
him of his leprosy." Naaman went to his master and told
him what the girl from Israel had said. "By all means, go,"
the king of Aram replied. "I will send a letter to the king of
Israel." So Naaman left.... The letter that he took to the king
of Israel read: "With this letter I am sending my servant
Naaman to you so that you may cure him of his leprosy."*

2 KINGS 5:1-6 NIV

Naaman was a big deal, yet he must have been a humble
man too—willing to listen to a mere servant girl from Israel.
Naaman was soon healed, and he gave God all the glory. Like
Naaman, we too should be humble when we seek answers
and healing from God, never unwilling to listen to the even
the meekest among us if they are pointing us to more faith
in and dependence on the one true God of miracles and
His perfect Word.

*Heavenly Father, I want to be a good listener
and follow You well. Please always keep
me humble and teachable. Amen.*

54

Praise and Pray All the Time

I will extol the LORD at all times; his praise will always be on my lips. I will glory in the LORD; let the afflicted hear and rejoice. Glorify the LORD with me; let us exalt his name together. I sought the LORD, and he answered me; he delivered me from all my fears. Those who look to him are radiant; their faces are never covered with shame.

PSALM 34:1-5 NIV

It can be hard to be careful with our words. But if praise to God is always on our lips like this psalm says, then there won't be much room for complaints or grumblings or foul language. Another scripture says, "Pray in the Spirit on all occasions with all kinds of prayers and requests" (Ephesians 6:18 NIV). When we do our best to remember these two scriptures, our minds and lips will be busy doing good things that fill us with hope instead of things that fill us with despair and lead us into trouble.

Heavenly Father, I want to be filled with great hope by choosing praise and prayer and keeping them in my mind and on my lips! Amen.

Hope and Help for Heavy Loads

*"Come to Me, all of you who work and have heavy
loads. I will give you rest. Follow My teachings and
learn from Me. I am gentle and do not have pride.
You will have rest for your souls. For My way of
carrying a load is easy and My load is not heavy."*
MATTHEW 11:28–30 NLV

Anytime something feels heavy or troubling in your life, Jesus
wants to help you with it. Another scripture says, "Give all
your worries to Him because He cares for you" (1 Peter 5:7
NLV). Aren't you glad when you're exhausted and struggling
and someone comes along and says, "Let me help you with
that"? That's what Jesus is saying here. Talk to Him about
every problem you have. Confess your sins to Him. Follow
His ways and learn from Him, and you will have the rest and
care you need.

*Dear Jesus, thank You for letting me come to You with
hard and heavy things. Thank You for taking them from
me and giving me rest and peace instead. I always
want to learn from You and live for You. Amen.*

Confession

*Come and listen, all you who fear God, and I will tell you
what he did for me. For I cried out to him for help, praising
him as I spoke. If I had not confessed the sin in my heart,
the Lord would not have listened. But God did listen!
He paid attention to my prayer. Praise God, who did not
ignore my prayer or withdraw his unfailing love from me.*

PSALM 66:16-20 NLT

God always hears our prayers because He is omniscient.
He sees all and knows all. But sometimes He doesn't seem
to pay attention to or answer our prayers. Sometimes that's
because we're holding on to sins in our lives rather than
admitting them to God and asking for His help to get rid of
them. James 5:13-16 talks about this subject as well. But there
is hope—because of Jesus' work on the cross, we can admit
all our sins, ask forgiveness, and be free of them. And when
we do, God pays attention to our prayers.

*Heavenly Father, thank You for Jesus' work on the
cross to free me from my sin. I admit and confess
my sin to You. Thank You for taking it away and
for paying attention to my prayers. Amen.*

Stronger Faith

At once the father cried out. He said with tears in his eyes,
"Lord, I have faith. Help my weak faith to be stronger!"

MARK 9:24 NLV

If you're struggling to understand what God is doing or not doing in response to what you're praying for, remember a story in the Bible from Mark 9. A father was asking Jesus for help for his son, who was possessed by an evil spirit. But the man struggled to imagine that Jesus really could do what he was asking. The father said to Jesus, "Have mercy on us and help us, if you can." Jesus replied, "What do you mean, 'If I can'? . . . Anything is possible if a person believes" (Mark 9:22–23 NLT). And the father said, "Lord, I have faith. Help my weak faith to be stronger!" When we pray, we must remember that God is able to do exactly what we ask and so much more! He may or may not answer the way we ask or expect, but no matter how God responds to our prayers, our main response to God should be, "Lord, I have faith. Help my weak faith to be stronger!"

Heavenly Father, please strengthen my faith
and hope in You, right now and increasingly
every day. Thank You! Amen.

Hope for When You Feel Persecuted

All day long those who hate me have walked on me. For there are many who fight against me with pride. When I am afraid, I will trust in You. I praise the Word of God. I have put my trust in God. I will not be afraid. What can only a man do to me? All day long they change my words to say what I did not say. They are always thinking of ways to hurt me. They go after me as in a fight.... Bring down the people in Your anger, O God.

PSALM 56:2–7 NLV

Maybe you can relate to the psalmist here. Maybe you feel like people in your life are hating you and walking all over you and twisting your words and trying to destroy you. But even as all these awful things are happening, the psalmist is putting his hope in God. He's remembering he doesn't need to be afraid of people when the one, true, all-powerful God is on His side. And that's what you can remember too.

Heavenly Father, when I feel persecuted, don't let me forget that You see and know what's going on. You will protect me and fight for me. Amen.

Sleep Soundly

You can go to bed without fear; you will lie down and sleep soundly. You need not be afraid of sudden disaster or the destruction that comes upon the wicked, for the LORD is your security.

PROVERBS 3:24-26 NLT

Whether we get enough or not, we all know how important sleep is. And no one can heal from any illness, injury, or pain—whether physical or emotional or both—unless they take time to let the body and mind rest. When you hope and trust in God, seeking Him and consistently following the wisdom of His Word, He will give you the rest and peace you need.

Heavenly Father, help me to remember how important rest is. Help me to be still and know that You are God! I hope in You and follow You. Please give me sweet and sound and healing slumber and Your peace that passes all understanding. Amen.

Shine a Light of Hope in the World

*Do all things without grumbling or disputing, that
you may be blameless and innocent, children of God
without blemish in the midst of a crooked and twisted
generation, among whom you shine as lights in the world.*
PHILIPPIANS 2:14-15 ESV

It's extremely difficult to do *all* things without grumbling or complaining. Yet that's what we should strive for. A good attitude is something we all need enormous help from God to cultivate. But if we can stay positive as we obey God and follow the plans He has for us, we shine as extra-bright lights to the sinful world around us. And just maybe people who don't yet trust in Jesus as their Savior will want to know more about God's love and peace because they see His light shining in our attitudes and actions.

*Heavenly Father, please help me to shine Your
light of hope in the darkness of sin around me in
this world. I want to shine brightly so others might
come to know Jesus as Savior too. Amen.*

None like the One True God

No pagan god is like you, O Lord. None can do what you do! All the nations you made will come and bow before you, Lord; they will praise your holy name. For you are great and perform wonderful deeds. You alone are God.

PSALM 86:8-10 NLT

When your hope is in the one true God, it is in exactly the right place—because nothing and no one else is like Him. The false gods and religions and spiritual ways of this world offer only empty, untrue hope. Only the one true God offers real grace and salvation through the gift of His Son, Jesus Christ, whom He sent as a sacrifice to pay for the sin of everyone who trusts in Him. Jesus alone covers our sin and offers eternal life and relationship with God, not because of anything we do but simply when we surrender, repent of sin, and believe in Him to save us. He said, "I am the way, the truth, and the life. No one can come to the Father except through me" (John 14:6 NLT).

Magnificent God, You alone are the one true God, and I bow before You and praise You! I thank You for saving me and giving me every reason to hope because Your Son, Jesus Christ, has paid for my sin. I trust in You alone. Amen.

Hope for Having a Child

Zechariah and Elizabeth were righteous in God's eyes, careful to obey all of the Lord's commandments and regulations. They had no children because Elizabeth was unable to conceive, and they were both very old.

LUKE 1:6-7 NLT

Elizabeth and her husband, Zechariah, both thought they were far too old to have children; but God sent the angel Gabriel to tell Zechariah that Elizabeth would have a son, and they should name him John. Zechariah didn't believe it. Because of his unbelief, God made him unable to speak. But soon Elizabeth became pregnant. " 'How kind the Lord is!' she exclaimed. 'He has taken away my disgrace of having no children' " (Luke 1:25 NLT).

Heavenly Father, remind me through the story of Elizabeth and Zechariah and their miracle son, John, that even when things seem totally impossible, there is always hope. You work in miraculous ways according to Your perfect will and perfect plans. Amen.

Don't Focus on Fears

*I will honor the Lord at all times. His praise will always
be in my mouth. My soul will be proud to tell about
the Lord. Let those who suffer hear it and be filled
with joy. Give great honor to the Lord with me. Let us
praise His name together. I looked for the Lord, and
He answered me. And He took away all my fears.
They looked to Him and their faces shined with joy.*

PSALM 34:1–5 NLV

What are you fearing right now? How are you battling those
fears and choosing not to focus on them? Fears grow bigger
in your mind if you let them have a lot of room in there. So
don't! Instead, give God a lot of room in your mind. Focus on
Him instead of fear by reading His Word, singing praises to
Him, and praying to Him. Ask Him to show Himself to you in
all kinds of ways. Then wait and see how He takes away all
your fears and replaces them with hope and peace and joy!

*Heavenly Father, please help me to take my focus
off my fears and put it on You instead. Fill my mind
and heart with hope and peace and joy because my
thoughts are on You and full of praise to You! Amen.*

Good Medicine

*A cheerful heart is good medicine, but a
broken spirit saps a person's strength.*
PROVERBS 17:22 NLT

Everyone has heard that "laughter is the best medicine." It's so true that doing our best to have a cheerful attitude and good sense of humor, even in the midst of struggle or pain or grief, has a huge impact on how quickly and well we heal from any kind of illness or injury. Depression, or a broken spirit, totally saps a person's strength—this scripture tells us so, and we've all either witnessed it in others or experienced it ourselves. So keep laughing. Keep looking for things to smile about and be grateful for, and ask God to show you when you can't see any yourself. And remember that "for the despondent, every day brings trouble; for the happy heart, life is a continual feast" (Proverbs 15:15 NLT).

*Heavenly Father, even in the worst of times,
please give me a supernaturally happy heart
and a good sense of humor. Help me to focus on
blessings. Use laughter and joy and gratitude
to help heal and restore me, please. Amen.*

Forget Not All His Benefits

*Praise the LORD, my soul; all my inmost being, praise
his holy name. Praise the LORD, my soul, and forget
not all his benefits—who forgives all your sins and
heals all your diseases, who redeems your life from
the pit and crowns you with love and compassion,
who satisfies your desires with good things so
that your youth is renewed like the eagle's.*

PSALM 103:1–5 NIV

If you're struggling with hopelessness or discouragement
today, have you forgotten all God's benefits to you? Don't
look around to see what others have been blessed with that
you have not. Look inwardly and at the life God has given
specifically to you, then thank Him for every blessing, for
even every single breath you take. You have life because
He has given it to you. And you have purpose and joy when
you live your life *in* Christ and *for* Christ, focusing on Him
above all else and praising Him for every good thing He gives
along your journey.

*Heavenly Father, please forgive me when I forget all
Your benefits to me. Help me to not compare my life
and blessings with the lives and blessings of others.
Instead, help me to live the unique life You have
given me with gratitude and for Your glory. Amen.*

Proven Faith

*Shadrach, Meshach and Abednego replied to him, "King
Nebuchadnezzar, we do not need to defend ourselves
before you in this matter. If we are thrown into the blazing
furnace, the God we serve is able to deliver us from
it, and he will deliver us from Your Majesty's hand."*

DANIEL 3:16-17 NIV

We prove that our faith in God is real when we keep on
trusting in God even if things don't go the way we hoped and
prayed for and were confident of at first. Shadrach, Meshach,
and Abednego were true heroes of the faith. They believed
without a doubt that God could save them from the blazing
furnace, but they went on to tell King Nebuchadnezzar, "Even
if he does not, we want you to know, Your Majesty, that we
will not serve your gods or worship the image of gold you
have set up" (Daniel 3:18 NIV).

*Heavenly Father, I want to prove that my faith in
You is 100 percent real. I will never worship anyone
but You, even if You don't answer my prayers the
way I know You can and hope You will. Amen.*

It's a Trap

*Yet true godliness with contentment is itself great wealth.
After all, we brought nothing with us when we came
into the world, and we can't take anything with us when
we leave it. So if we have enough food and clothing, let
us be content. But people who long to be rich fall into
temptation and are trapped by many foolish and harmful
desires that plunge them into ruin and destruction. For
the love of money is the root of all kinds of evil. And
some people, craving money, have wandered from the
true faith and pierced themselves with many sorrows.*

1 TIMOTHY 6:6-10 NLT

The Bible is clear that it's total foolishness to put our hope
in money and wealth. It's a trap. And those who get caught
in this trap often venture into all kinds of sin and harmful
things that result in their total destruction. We must ask God
to help us put all our hope in Him rather than in wealth and
worldly success. He will give us goals that match up with His
good plans for our lives, according to the gifts and talents
He has given us.

*Heavenly Father, please help me to never make my hopes
and goals about money; I want them to be about serving
You and giving You glory! Please help me keep my focus
on all the best things You have planned for me. Amen.*

The Privilege of Being Called by His Name

If you are insulted because you bear the name of Christ, you will be blessed, for the glorious Spirit of God rests upon you. If you suffer, however, it must not be for murder, stealing, making trouble, or prying into other people's affairs. But it is no shame to suffer for being a Christian. Praise God for the privilege of being called by his name!

1 PETER 4:14-16 NLT

The wounds from the words of others who ridicule you for your faith in Jesus can feel so painful and deep. But there is healing in the words of scripture: "God blesses you when people mock you and persecute you and lie about you and say all sorts of evil things against you because you are my followers. Be happy about it! Be very glad! For a great reward awaits you in heaven. And remember, the ancient prophets were persecuted in the same way" (Matthew 5:11-12 NLT).

Dear Jesus, I will follow You no matter what anyone says against me. I am so grateful for the privilege of being called Your follower—a Christian. I can't deny that words can hurt sometimes, though, so please remind me of Your promises. Heal my pain, and help me to hold my head high as I put my hope in You! Amen.

God Knit You Together

*For you created my inmost being; you knit me together
in my mother's womb. I praise you because I am fearfully
and wonderfully made; your works are wonderful,
I know that full well. My frame was not hidden from
you when I was made in the secret place, when I was
woven together in the depths of the earth. Your eyes saw
my unformed body; all the days ordained for me were
written in your book before one of them came to be.*

PSALM 139:13–16 NIV

No one knows you better than the one true Creator God
who made you. He planned you and all the days of your life
before you were even born. The God of all the universe put
every piece of you together, and He loves you most and wants
what's best for you in all things. Since all these things are
true, don't ever let anyone put you down or steal your hope.

*Heavenly Father, when I start to lose hope and
feel discouraged, please help me remember
that You designed me and the plans for my life
in great detail and with great love. Amen.*

Maker of Mountains

For the LORD is the one who shaped the mountains, stirs up the winds, and reveals his thoughts to mankind. He turns the light of dawn into darkness and treads on the heights of the earth. The LORD God of Heaven's Armies is his name!

AMOS 4:13 NLT

Time in the mountains is both peaceful and overwhelming—the mountains remind us how incredibly small and weak we humans are in comparison to the size and strength of such majestic landforms. Can you imagine God easily walking around on top of them? The Bible says He can! When you are facing problems or fears that seem like mountains that are far too massive for you to handle, picture the Lord God of all walking on top of them and then reaching down His hand to help you over them.

Heavenly Father, You are great and mighty! You are able to help me overcome any problems that might seem like insurmountable mountains in my life. Please keep holding my hand and helping me over them. Amen.

His Heart Overflowed with Compassion

*A funeral procession was coming out as he approached
the village gate. The young man who had died was a
widow's only son, and a large crowd from the village was
with her. When the Lord saw her, his heart overflowed with
compassion. "Don't cry!" he said. Then he walked over to
the coffin and touched it, and the bearers stopped. "Young
man," he said, "I tell you, get up." Then the dead boy sat up
and began to talk! And Jesus gave him back to his mother.*

LUKE 7:12–15 NLT

In Bible times, if a woman had no husband and no sons, she
was in a dangerous situation. It was nearly impossible for a
woman to provide for herself and protect herself without a
man back then. So when Jesus saw this widow whose son had
just died, He had extra concern for her. "His heart overflowed
with compassion." Then He brought her dead son back to
life and gave him back to his mother. Can you imagine her
extreme joy and relief and total awe and gratitude for Jesus?

*Dear Jesus, thank You for Your miracles and Your
compassion! You care so much about people who
are in awful situations. Help me to trust in Your
care, knowing that You can provide healing here
on earth and ultimately healing in heaven forever.
Help me also to care for others like You do. Amen.*

Your Strength and Refuge

But as for me, I will sing about your power. Each morning I will sing with joy about your unfailing love. For you have been my refuge, a place of safety when I am in distress. O my Strength, to you I sing praises, for you, O God, are my refuge, the God who shows me unfailing love.

PSALM 59:16-17 NLT

Nothing ever compares to God as your ultimate source of strength and refuge. His power is far beyond any kind of human strength. When you choose to focus on His power and even sing about it in praise and worship, you can be filled with great hope and courage. You can remember you never need to depend on your own strength when you have God with you. He will not fail you.

Heavenly Father, my strength and refuge, I love You and praise You and put my hope in You. I know You are strong enough to do anything to help whenever I need it. Amen.

He Is Risen!

Then the angel spoke to the women. "Don't be afraid!" he said. "I know you are looking for Jesus, who was crucified. He isn't here! He is risen from the dead, just as he said would happen. Come, see where his body was lying. And now, go quickly and tell his disciples that he has risen from the dead, and he is going ahead of you to Galilee. You will see him there. Remember what I have told you."

MATTHEW 28:5-9 NLT

Can you imagine being one of these women, these dear friends of Jesus? It had to be the most wonderful surprise ever to hear the angel's news and then meet up with Jesus, who was not dead but alive again! That powerful news is what we still trust today. Jesus is not dead. *He is alive!*

Dear Jesus, I believe You died to save me from my sin, but You did not stay dead. You are alive! You are my hope and the hope of the whole world. Amen.

Train for Godliness

Train yourself for godliness; for while bodily training is of some value, godliness is of value in every way, as it holds promise for the present life and also for the life to come. The saying is trustworthy and deserving of full acceptance. For to this end we toil and strive, because we have our hope set on the living God, who is the Savior of all people, especially of those who believe.

1 TIMOTHY 4:7–10 ESV

Struggling to maintain good health in an aging body in a world that glamorizes top physical fitness can make you feel hopeless. Of course we need to do our best to take good care of our bodies and health, but too many in our society worship physical fitness like a god. Ask God for wisdom and discipline for healthy living, eating, and exercise; but even more, ask God for wisdom and discipline for healthy training in godliness—spending time studying and learning God's Word and letting yourself be shaped by it, both for now and for eternity.

Heavenly Father, please help me with my physical health, but even more please help me with my spiritual health. My hope is not in my earthly body. My hope is in You and the eternal life You promise. Amen.

Hope for Something New

*"But forget all that—it is nothing compared to what
I am going to do. For I am about to do something
new. See, I have already begun! Do you not see
it? I will make a pathway through the wilderness.
I will create rivers in the dry wasteland."*

ISAIAH 43:18-19 NLT

In this scripture, God was telling His people to forget the hard
times of the past and let Him bring them into something new
and good. Do you have hard times you need to forget too? We
all do. Maybe you feel like last year was just awful, and now
you feel worried about the new year ahead. But just be glad
last year (or whatever it is that you're glad is over) is done,
and let it go! Let God help you every moment of every day.
Let His wonderful grace cover you. Let His amazing love,
joy, and peace fill you up. Let Him restore your hope. Let
Him protect you and lead you. Let Him do the new things
He wants to do in and through you.

*Heavenly Father, help me to focus with great hope and
confidence on the awesome new things You are doing.
You are in me, and my life is from You and for You.
Please fill me up with Your good blessings. Amen.*

Hope from Angels

Are not all the angels spirits who work for God? They are sent out to help those who are to be saved from the punishment of sin.

HEBREWS 1:14 NLV

Do you think much about angels? It's important that what we believe about them comes not from the world's ideas but from the truth in God's Word. This scripture shows us that we can trust that angels absolutely exist, and we can put hope in how they will minister to us. They are spirits who work for God, and they are sent to help all who trust in Jesus as Savior. The fact of their existence and mission is amazing to think about! We can confidently ask God to send His angels to care for us and rescue us—and others—in any kind of trouble.

Heavenly Father, thank You that angels are real. Please send them to me when I need them. Thank You for the ways You care for me and protect me through the help of angels. Amen.

Goodness and Mercy All Your Days

Surely goodness and mercy shall follow me all the days of my life, and I shall dwell in the house of the LORD forever.

PSALM 23:6 ESV

The psalmist David didn't say *only* goodness and mercy would follow him all his days. But he did say they *would* follow him. And they will follow you today as well, even in whatever struggle or pain or illness you are going through. As you endure hardship, look specifically for the goodness and mercy you see in each day, even when heartache and confusion and suffering are raging at their worst. Cling to that goodness and mercy. Write it down. Pray in gratitude for it. Sing praise about it. Remember it tomorrow, even while you look for the new goodness and mercy and grace God will give you. He will carry you through, until one day you are dwelling in His house forever.

Heavenly Father, help me to notice and appreciate each and every bit of goodness and mercy You are constantly giving me, even in the midst of trials. I praise You and thank You for it all, and I trust in You to continue to give it. Amen.

Give God All the Credit and Praise

If anyone wants to be proud, he should be proud of what
the Lord has done. It is not what a man thinks and says
of himself that is important. It is what God thinks of him.

2 CORINTHIANS 10:17–18 NLV

Our hope and pride should never be in ourselves and our own accomplishments. Of course we feel happy when we achieve or complete something great. And that's wonderful! But we must never forget to always give God credit for each good thing we do. He deserves every bit of praise and worship, because He is the One who gives us all our gifts and abilities.

Heavenly Father, please help me never to hope or
have pride in myself, but rather remember You are
the One who gives me every reason to feel proud
and have hope. Every good thing comes from You,
and You are so generous! I'm so grateful! Amen.

How Sweet Is God's Word

O, how I love Your Law! It is what I think about all through the day. Your Word makes me wiser than those who hate me, for it is always with me. I have better understanding than all my teachers because I think about Your Law. I have a better understanding than those who are old because I obey Your Word. I have kept my feet from every sinful way so that I may keep Your Word. I have not turned away from Your Law, for You Yourself have taught me. How sweet is Your Word to my taste! It is sweeter than honey to my mouth! I get understanding from Your Law and so I hate every false way.

PSALM 119:97–104 NLV

This scripture from Psalms shows how we should think of God's Word and praise Him for it. The Bible is living and active (Hebrews 4:12) and is inspired by God and useful in every area of our lives (2 Timothy 3:16). Like the psalmist, we should have great love and enthusiasm for God's Word, recognizing how blessed we are to learn from it, follow it, and receive hope from it, with the help of the Holy Spirit.

Heavenly Father, thank You for the gift of Your Word! Help me to value it the way I should. Remind me of this psalm every day. I sing and pray it to You right now with all of my heart. Amen.

Jesus Gives Us Peace

"Peace I leave with you. My peace I give to you.
I do not give peace to you as the world gives.
Do not let your hearts be troubled or afraid."

JOHN 14:27 NLV

Don't let the troubles of the world make you feel hopeless about ever having any peace. Jesus has given you a supernatural peace that transcends all understanding (Philippians 4:6-7). Peaceful things here on earth—a relaxing beach, a quiet afternoon, a laid-back get-together with family and friends—sure are nice, but they are not the deep, constant, miraculous peace that only Jesus can give. Whenever you feel troubled or afraid, ask the Holy Spirit to fill you with the perfect peace of Jesus.

Dear Jesus, anytime I am troubled or afraid, please calm me down by reminding me of Your perfect peace. Amen.

Let Yourself Lament

*I have cried until the tears no longer come; my
heart is broken. My spirit is poured out in agony
as I see the desperate plight of my people.*
LAMENTATIONS 2:11 NLT

In the book of Lamentations, Jeremiah wrote down all of his sadness and pain over the destruction of the city of Jerusalem resulting from the people's turning away from God. The word *lamentation* means an expression of sorrow. For healing from heartache, we also might find it helpful to write down our feelings, telling God all about them and allowing Him to comfort and strengthen us again. We might want to share our lamentation with trusted loved ones as well, because God can use their care to help us.

Heavenly Father, help me to remember it's okay to acknowledge my feelings of heartache. Help me to share them with You and with people who love me. I trust that You will bring me the comfort and encouragement and healing and hope I need. Amen.

Ask for Good Gifts

"Ask and it will be given to you; seek and you will find; knock and the door will be opened to you. For everyone who asks receives; the one who seeks finds; and to the one who knocks, the door will be opened. Which of you, if your son asks for bread, will give him a stone? Or if he asks for a fish, will give him a snake? If you, then, though you are evil, know how to give good gifts to your children, how much more will your Father in heaven give good gifts to those who ask him!"

MATTHEW 7:7–11 NIV

God never tires of hearing of hearing from you (Romans 12:12; Ephesians 6:18; 1 Thessalonians 5:16–18). He's your wonderful heavenly Dad! His Word encourages you to pray about absolutely everything and ask Him to bless you. So keep talking to Him constantly! He loves you; He loves to listen to you; He loves to give you good things.

Heavenly Father, thank You for listening to me and giving me good gifts! Please bless me in the ways You know are best for me. Amen.

Hope from the Heroes

Faith shows the reality of what we hope for; it is the evidence of things we cannot see. Through their faith, the people in days of old earned a good reputation.

HEBREWS 11:1-2 NLT

Let Hebrews 11 strengthen you today. It defines what our faith is—being sure of what we hope for and certain of what we do not see—and gives us an incredible summary of so many heroes who've gone before us, holding to their faith. Their example inspires us to keep on believing and being obedient to God, even when we can't see all of His plans or the final result. Think of how you'd like your name to be remembered among your family and friends and future generations as one who never gave up on God. Though we cannot see all that He is doing right now, we absolutely will one day soon.

Heavenly Father, please inspire me with renewed hope as I read about the heroes of the faith in Your Word. I want to persevere like they did. Amen.

The Plans of the Lord Stand Forever

The Lord brings the plans of nations to nothing. He wrecks the plans of the people. The plans of the Lord stand forever. The plans of His heart stand through the future of all people. Happy is the nation whose God is the Lord. Happy are the people He has chosen for His own.
PSALM 33:10-12 NLV

Worry and fear that others might have bad intentions toward you can make you feel helpless and hopeless. So never forget that God wrecks the plans of the people if He wants to. He can wreck any malicious plan that someone might be plotting against you. And if He does allow something bad to happen to you, He has a greater plan for making you stronger because of it and turning it into something good instead. Romans 8:28 (NLV) promises, "God makes all things work together for the good of those who love Him and are chosen to be a part of His plan."

Heavenly Father, I believe You can wreck any bad plan or turn it into good in the way that only You can do. Your plans are always the best, and I trust You! Amen.

Every Step You Take

Let the Holy Spirit lead you in each step. Then you will not please your sinful old selves. The things our old selves want to do are against what the Holy Spirit wants. The Holy Spirit does not agree with what our sinful old selves want.

GALATIANS 5:16-17 NLV

Think of times when you've needed to be led step by step. Maybe on a really tough hike in the woods or mountains. Or maybe in physical therapy when recovering from an injury or surgery. Or maybe in navigating your way through grief. Really think about how every day of your life you need to be led in each step to live a life that is pleasing to God. All on your own, you will do what your old sinful self wants. But with God's Holy Spirit in you, you can let Him lead you to do what He wants for you. And since He made you and loves you more than anyone else, you can trust that what He wants is always best for you!

Holy Spirit, please lead me in each step of my life. When I start to go my own way, please guide me back to You! I know what You want for me is always what's best. Amen.

Put to the Test

*"For the Lord your God is putting you to the test
to see if you love the Lord your God with all your
heart and with all your soul. Follow the Lord your
God and fear Him. Keep His Laws, and listen to
His voice. Work for Him, and hold on to Him."*

DEUTERONOMY 13:3–4 NLV

Don't let tests in life discourage you. Remember that God
allows them at times to see if your faith in Him alone is real
and if you love Him with all your heart and soul. These are
tests you sure do want to pass with flying colors! So listen to
God, obey Him, follow Him, and work for Him. Hold on tight
to faith in the one true God—the only One worthy of faith—
and watch how He reveals His faithfulness to you in return.

*Heavenly Father, please help me to have hope even
in the midst of difficult tests that prove how much
I love You and believe in You. I never want to stop
holding on to faith in You and You alone. Amen.*

David's Confidence

But David said to Saul, "Your servant. . .has killed both the lion and the bear. And this Philistine who has not gone through our religious act will be like one of them. For he has made fun of the armies of the living God." And David said, "The Lord Who saved me from the foot of the lion and from the foot of the bear, will save me from the hand of this Philistine." Saul said to David, "Go, and may the Lord be with you."
1 SAMUEL 17:34, 36–37 NLV

David was sure he could fight the giant Goliath. He knew God had helped him fight lions and bears in the past, and so God would also help him fight the Philistine giant whom everyone else was afraid of. Let David's example encourage you. Sometimes you simply need to remember all the ways God has helped you fight and win in the past, and that act of remembrance can give you everything you need to let God help you win whatever battle you need to fight right now.

Heavenly Father, when I face a battle, fill me with hope and confidence by reminding me how You have made me victorious in the past. Amen.

Overpowering Hope

We want you to know for sure about those who have died. You have no reason to have sorrow as those who have no hope. We believe that Jesus died and then came to life again. Because we believe this, we know that God will bring to life again all those who belong to Jesus.

1 THESSALONIANS 4:13-14 NLV

If you've experienced the loss of a family member or friend, you know the pain and sorrow can be excruciating. But even while you ache and grieve, you can have hope that overpowers the pain and sadness; because if your loved one trusted Jesus, then they will be brought to life again just as He rose again. The promise of eternal life brings extraordinary comfort and hope—and it should motivate us to share the good news of Jesus with others. Just like God does, we should want all people to be saved from sin (1 Timothy 2:4).

Heavenly Father, remind me every moment of the hope of Jesus to overpower the pain of grief and loss. Help me to share the Good News, and help others to receive You as Savior so we all can be raised to life again with You forever. Amen.

Trust Him to Multiply

Another of his disciples, Andrew, Simon Peter's brother,
spoke up, "Here is a boy with five small barley loaves and
two small fish, but how far will they go among so many?"

JOHN 6:8-9 NIV

"How far will they go among so many?" Jesus' disciple Andrew asked. We can relate when we wonder how our meager provisions or our finances—or even our energy—can possibly meet the great demands in our lives. With our human limitations and weaknesses, we can feel utterly hopeless. But just as Jesus took five loaves and two fish to feed multitudes of people with loads left over, God is able to take anything we have and turn it into so much more to meet our needs and the needs of others. Offer Him everything you have, and then trust Him to multiply it in miraculous ways.

Dear Jesus, remind me that You can take my smallest
offering and turn it into far, far above and beyond what
I need and hope for. I praise and thank You! Amen.

The Unchanging One

"I am the LORD, and I do not change."

MALACHI 3:6 NLT

Some people love and thrive on variety and change in life, while others dread it. Change, especially sudden change, can make people feel hopeless and out of control. And so the peace and assurance that come from focusing on God's unchanging nature are especially refreshing and uplifting. "Jesus Christ is the same yesterday, today, and forever" (Hebrews 13:8 NLT). Nothing and no one else in all creation can make that claim. His "plans stand firm forever; his intentions can never be shaken" (Psalm 33:11 NLT). Moreover, "He never changes or casts a shifting shadow" (James 1:17 NLT).

Heavenly Father, when too much change makes me feel panicky and hopeless, help me to cling more tightly to Your unchanging, eternal nature. You are sovereign and good and in control of every detail of all Your perfect plans. Fill me with Your consistent, persistent peace. Amen.

Questions for Job

"Where were you when I began building the earth? Tell Me, if you have understanding. Who decided how big it was to be, since you know? Who looked to see if it was as big as it should be? What was it built upon? Who laid its first stone, when the morning stars sang together and all the sons of God called out for joy? Who shut up the sea with doors, when it rushed out from its secret place?"

JOB 38:4-8 NLV

God asks Job some rhetorical questions that He knows Job knows the answers to. The questioning is a reminder to Job that God alone is all-knowing, all-powerful, amazing, and every other awesome adjective. There is only one true God who has extraordinary power to create and control all things. No matter what is feeling so hard and overwhelming in your life right now, you can have great hope in our almighty Creator God who is also your heavenly Father, your loving Savior, Jesus Christ, and the powerful Holy Spirit within you. Worship Him today and every day and trust Him with your life, because He alone is able to do absolutely anything!

Heavenly Father, You are the awesome answer to every question about who creates and has power and does all good things! I am so blessed to hope in You and worship You! Amen.

Because the Lord Is Your Shepherd

The Lord is my shepherd, I lack nothing. He makes me lie down in green pastures, he leads me beside quiet waters, he refreshes my soul. He guides me along the right paths for his name's sake. Even though I walk through the darkest valley, I will fear no evil, for you are with me; your rod and your staff, they comfort me.

PSALM 23:1–4 NIV

The Lord God is your Shepherd leading you and giving you everything you need. Let the words of this well-known psalm infuse you with hope and strength and courage. Memorize it, and repeat it throughout your day; let it encourage you in the midst of whatever you are facing!

Dear Lord, because You lead me and care for me, I have nothing to fear. Not one thing! Thank You, thank You, my loving Shepherd! Amen.

Stronger Together

I long to visit you so I can bring you some spiritual gift that will help you grow strong in the Lord. When we get together, I want to encourage you in your faith, but I also want to be encouraged by yours.

ROMANS 1:11-12 NLT

Think of your family and friends who also follow Jesus and aren't afraid to show it. With great gratitude, focus on what a blessing they are. We all need each other, and together we make each other stronger. We spread hope and encouragement to one another by sharing the gifts we've received from the Holy Spirit, by telling how God is working in our lives, by praying for each other, and by reminding each other of the truths of the Bible.

Heavenly Father, thank You for the dear people in my life who help make my faith in You stronger every day. Help me to encourage and make them stronger too. Amen.

Be Generous

"Give, and it will be given to you. You will have more than enough. It can be pushed down and shaken together and it will still run over as it is given to you. The way you give to others is the way you will receive in return."

LUKE 6:38 NLV

We are called to share God's love and hope with others by being generous. It takes courage to give away what we have, because we have to trust that we will still have what we need. But there's no need to fret. God will always supply enough for our own needs as we help provide for the needs of others. The Bible promises it! The more we give, the more God will give us! He loves to reward us when we share the gifts that ultimately always come from Him.

Heavenly Father, please help me to be a cheerful, generous giver. I want to share Your hope and love by helping provide for others' needs in Your name. I trust that You will always bless and provide for me too. Amen.

A Rich Life

He has made your lives rich in every way. Now you have power to speak for Him. He gave you good understanding. This shows that what I told you about Christ and what He could do for you has been done in your lives. You have the gifts of the Holy Spirit that you need while you wait for the Lord Jesus Christ to come again. Christ will keep you strong until He comes again.

1 CORINTHIANS 1:4-8 NLV

What are the many ways God has made your life "rich in every way"? Do you have a gratitude journal in which to list them and focus on them? Thanking and praising God for His goodness to you fills you with hope for more of His goodness. Ask Him to show you the gifts of the Holy Spirit that He has given you. Let Him tell you how He wants you to use them specifically in this world until He comes again. Jesus knows you and loves you and will keep you strong until the day He returns!

Heavenly Father, thank You for making me rich in every way. Please keep me strong and help me to use these riches You have given me in the ways You want me to. Amen.

Lessons from Habakkuk

This is the special word which Habakkuk the man of God saw. O Lord, how long must I call for help before You will hear? I cry out to You, "We are being hurt!" But You do not save us.

HABAKKUK 1:1–2 NLV

We can all relate to asking God questions and feeling confused. Sometimes we wonder why we have to wait so long on Him or why He doesn't answer our prayers the way we hoped. Habakkuk was a prophet of God who had a lot of questions. We can learn from him that even though he never got the exact answers he wanted from God, he got answers that reminded him of this: God is all-powerful and completely good, and He will work out His perfect plans in His perfect timing. We must continue to trust what Habakkuk learned.

Heavenly Father, like Habakkuk, even when I have questions and feel confused, I want to be able to say, "Yet I will have joy in the Lord. I will be glad in the God Who saves me" (Habakkuk 3:18 NLV). Amen.

Deep Roots

*As you have put your trust in Christ Jesus the Lord
to save you from the punishment of sin, now let Him
lead you in every step. Have your roots planted deep
in Christ. Grow in Him. Get your strength from Him.
Let Him make you strong in the faith as you have been
taught. Your life should be full of thanks to Him.*

COLOSSIANS 2:6-7 NLV

How strong is your faith in Christ? Can it always get stronger?
Absolutely! As you let Him lead you in every step through
the work of the Holy Spirit, your roots will grow deeper and
deeper into Him. The deeper the roots of a tree go, the stronger it is. The deeper its roots grow, the harder it is for the tree
to fall. The same goes for you. The deeper your roots grow
in Jesus, the stronger you are in your faith and the harder it
is for any hard thing in life to make you fall.

*Dear Jesus, please keep me growing deeper
roots into You. Strengthen my faith each day
as You lead me in every step. Amen.*

God Will Never Leave You or Let You Be Alone

God has said, "I will never leave you or let you be alone." So we can say for sure, "The Lord is my Helper. I am not afraid of anything man can do to me."
HEBREWS 13:5-6 NLV

Being alone during a difficult time can make the situation feel practically unbearable. But to have even just one devoted friend or loved one by your side can make all the difference in the world. Praise God for those precious people! Yet there are times in life when we have to do some difficult things without another person by our side for support. Yet even then, we are never truly alone because of the Holy Spirit within us. God has promised He never leaves us and never lets us be alone. He knows our situation and every thought and fear and need. He hears our every prayer. And He will answer in amazing ways to always show Himself as our Helper.

Heavenly Father, I believe You never leave me or let me be alone. Thank You for those times when You provide dear people to stay right by my side supporting me. And thank You for those times when You provide supernatural comfort and companionship. I'm grateful for Your constant presence in my life. Amen.

Was It an Angel?

"Last night an angel of the God to whom I belong and whom I serve stood beside me, and he said, 'Don't be afraid, Paul.'"

ACTS 27:23-24 NLT

Has a stranger ever said something to you that was exactly what you needed to hear? Maybe someone comforted you. Maybe someone reassured and encouraged you. What if that someone was really an angel sent by God? It really could have been, especially if you'd never seen the person before and you've never seen them since! Whenever you have an experience like that, notice and thank God for it. Whether it was an angel or not, God used that someone in your life to help you. You can trust that He will always send the right people or angels to you with exactly the right words and help—exactly when you need them!

Heavenly Father, thank You for the times You have used people I don't even know to help me and encourage me. You give hope and help through all kinds of people and in all kinds of ways. Amen.

Hope in the Midst of Uncertainty

Confused and disturbed, Mary tried to
think what the angel could mean.

LUKE 1:29 NLT

Imagine being Mary—the shock of suddenly becoming miraculously pregnant after being told by an angel that she had been chosen to carry the Son of God! Mary could have given in to anxiety and fear, but instead she chose hope and praise and a humble willingness to be used by God however He led. Mary's response—"I am the Lord's servant. May everything you have said about me come true" (Luke 1:38 NLT)—and her song found in Luke 1:46-55, inspire all of us to cling to hope in the midst of great uncertainty. May we say, no matter our circumstances, "Oh, how my soul praises the Lord. How my spirit rejoices in God my Savior!" (verses 46-47 NLT).

Heavenly Father, no matter what You ask me to do in life, no matter how hard it might be, I want to have the kind of response Mary had. Please help me. I want to be willing to do anything for You and praise You through all of it. I know You are good and ask only good things of me. Amen.

Well Equipped

Put on the full armor of God, so that when the day of evil comes, you may be able to stand your ground, and after you have done everything, to stand. Stand firm then, with the belt of truth buckled around your waist, with the breastplate of righteousness in place, and with your feet fitted with the readiness that comes from the gospel of peace. In addition to all this, take up the shield of faith, with which you can extinguish all the flaming arrows of the evil one. Take the helmet of salvation and the sword of the Spirit, which is the word of God.

EPHESIANS 6:13-17 NIV

God knows we will have battles in this world—battles with our enemy, the devil, and the spiritual forces of evil. But God never leaves us helpless or hopeless in these battles. We have the Holy Spirit in us, and He gives us armor and weapons to be protected and ready to fight! Think about these verses when you feel under attack, and remember God will never let the devil defeat you.

Heavenly Father, thank You for equipping me in every battle against evil. I am strong and able to fight because of You! Amen.

God Did Not Abandon Them

"But our ancestors were proud and stubborn, and they paid no attention to your commands. They refused to obey and did not remember the miracles you had done for them.... But you are a God of forgiveness, gracious and merciful, slow to become angry, and rich in unfailing love. You did not abandon them, even when they made an idol shaped like a calf and said, 'This is your god who brought you out of Egypt!' They committed terrible blasphemies. But in your great mercy you did not abandon them."

NEHEMIAH 9:16-19 NLT

Be reminded by God's Word of how patient and good our God is, even when His people treat Him horribly. Even then He is forgiving and kind and loving. He provides for His people and gives us His Holy Spirit to teach us. This scripture might be about ancient times and ancient people, but we can apply the truth in it to our own lives today.

Heavenly Father, knowing that You don't abandon Your people fills me with hope. Thank You for Your amazing grace and compassionate mercy. Amen.

With God, All Things Are Possible

Jesus said to his disciples, "Truly, I say to you, only with difficulty will a rich person enter the kingdom of heaven. Again I tell you, it is easier for a camel to go through the eye of a needle than for a rich person to enter the kingdom of God." When the disciples heard this, they were greatly astonished, saying, "Who then can be saved?" But Jesus looked at them and said, "With man this is impossible, but with God all things are possible."

MATTHEW 19:23-26 ESV

Maybe you are praying for someone you love to trust in Jesus as their Savior, but they keep refusing to admit their need for Him. Their salvation might seem absolutely impossible, but keep on hoping and praying for them and loving them anyway. Remember the promise in these words of Jesus from Matthew 19 that "with God all things are possible."

Heavenly Father, I pray for my friends and loved ones who seem so unwilling to trust in You as Savior. Help me to remember that nothing is impossible for You! Amen.

Hope in the Midst of Fear and Anxiety

*God gave us a spirit not of fear but of
power and love and self-control.*
2 TIMOTHY 1:7 ESV

When fear and anxiety are creeping up on you, what good, healthy things help calm you down and comfort you and make you feel safe? Bible verses you've memorized should be a top go-to, like 2 Timothy 1:7, reminding you that God has given you a spirit of power, love, and self-control to defeat any spirit of fear. Another to memorize and repeat is Psalm 56:3–4 (NLV): "When I am afraid, I will trust in You. I praise the Word of God. I have put my trust in God. I will not be afraid." God's Word is powerful to help us when we feel anxiety and fear.

*Heavenly Father, thank You for Your Word that I can
remember and repeat when I need to focus on Your
power and love. Please take my anxiety and fear and
replace them with Your hope and peace. Amen.*

Hope Because of Friendship

Two people are better off than one, for they can help each other succeed. If one person falls, the other can reach out and help. But someone who falls alone is in real trouble. Likewise, two people lying close together can keep each other warm. But how can one be warm alone? A person standing alone can be attacked and defeated, but two can stand back-to-back and conquer. Three are even better, for a triple-braided cord is not easily broken.

ECCLESIASTES 4:9–12 NLT

Friendship is so important to encourage us and bring us hope. It's one of God's greatest gifts! In friendship, we help each other and support each other and protect each other and stand against enemies together too. Plus, it's just so much fun to have good friends to spend time with and laugh with! That's God's extra-special blessing on top. He gives us so much joy through good friendships. What a wonderful heavenly Father we have!

Heavenly Father, thank You for the gift of good friendships that encourage me and fill me with hope and love and joy! Please help my friends and I grow closer to each other, but most of all closer to You! Amen.

Rejoice in Confident Hope

Don't just pretend to love others. Really love them. Hate what is wrong. Hold tightly to what is good. Love each other with genuine affection, and take delight in honoring each other. Never be lazy, but work hard and serve the Lord enthusiastically. Rejoice in our confident hope. Be patient in trouble, and keep on praying.

ROMANS 12:9-12 NLT

Paul's instructions here in Romans 12 sum up the Christian life so well. We all need to compare our lives to this scripture regularly. Are we truly loving other people? Hating what is wrong? Holding tightly to what is good? Loving others with real affection and delighting in honoring each other? Working hard without laziness? Serving the Lord enthusiastically? Rejoicing in confident hope? Being patient in trouble? Praying all the time? Where your answers are *yes*, celebrate and worship God for His grace in growing the fruit of the Spirit in you! Where your answers are *no* or need work, admit your struggles to God and ask for His help to improve.

Heavenly Father, please help me to live my life as You have instructed in Your Word. Affirm and encourage me in the ways I'm doing well, and correct me where I need to change and improve. Amen.

God Is Always There

Where can I go from your Spirit? Where can I flee from your presence? If I go up to the heavens, you are there; if I make my bed in the depths, you are there. If I rise on the wings of the dawn, if I settle on the far side of the sea, even there your hand will guide me, your right hand will hold me fast. If I say, "Surely the darkness will hide me and the light become night around me," even the darkness will not be dark to you; the night will shine like the day, for darkness is as light to you.

PSALM 139:7-12 NIV

No matter how hard or painful your circumstance, you are never alone in it. God's presence through His Holy Spirit never leaves you. As hard as it is for our minds to comprehend it, He is omnipresent—everywhere at all times. He knows your every thought, hears your every cry, sees your every tear. He will hold your hand and guide you, so keep your hope in Him and don't let go.

Heavenly Father, I trust You are here with me right in this moment and in every moment through Your Holy Spirit. You know my hardship and pain. I trust that Your hand is guiding me through it. I won't let go. Amen.

Hope like the Poor Widow

Jesus sat down near the collection box in the Temple and watched as the crowds dropped in their money. Many rich people put in large amounts. Then a poor widow came and dropped in two small coins. Jesus called his disciples to him and said, "I tell you the truth, this poor widow has given more than all the others who are making contributions. For they gave a tiny part of their surplus, but she, poor as she is, has given everything she had to live on."

MARK 12:41-44 NLT

Clearly, this poor widow had great hope and trust in God. Not many of us can say we would do the same as she did and readily give God our last two pennies with total faith in His provision, despite total uncertainty of what would come next. In the Christian faith, the humblest individuals are the true heroes. This poor widow is a role model for real hope in God—giving to Him and trusting Him to provide for our every need in every uncertainty.

Heavenly Father, help me to hope in You like the poor widow did. I want to be willing to give everything I have to You, trusting You to provide everything I need. Amen.

God Is Always Stronger

*The One Who lives in you is stronger
than the one who is in the world.*

1 JOHN 4:4 NLV

The world can feel absolutely upside down these days. We have an enemy, the devil, who loves to spread sin and evil as much as he can (1 Peter 5:8; 1 John 5:19). Yet even when things seem out of control in the world around you, you always have hope and power and strength because of God's Holy Spirit living in you. Memorize 1 John 4:4 and then put it on repeat in your mind. God is *always* stronger than the devil. God never leaves you and will help you fight and win against any evil plan the enemy has against you.

Heavenly Father, don't let me forget that You are always stronger within me than the evil one who is in the world. Give me strength and courage and hope and confidence as I remember the power of Your Word and Your Holy Spirit within me. Amen.

Hope for Forgiveness

*"If you forgive those who sin against you, your heavenly
Father will forgive you. But if you refuse to forgive
others, your Father will not forgive your sins."*

MATTHEW 6:14-15 NLT

There is no hope for forgiveness for us if we don't forgive
others. It's not always easy to do, but the Bible is clear that
it's a big deal. Jesus said that God won't forgive our sins if we
don't forgive others. And we know how much we need Him
to forgive our sins and mistakes! Because we are forgiven so
generously through Jesus' work on the cross, we should want
to forgive generously as well.

*Dear Jesus, when I struggle to forgive, help me
to think about how thankful I am that You forgive
my sin. I want to follow Your example. Amen.*

No Greater Hope

For God so loved the world that he gave his
one and only Son, that whoever believes in
him shall not perish but have eternal life.

JOHN 3:16 NIV

John 3:16 is one of the most famous and popular verses in all of the Bible. Because it is so well known, sometimes we overlook it or forget its significance. But we really need to stop and dwell on it at times, for it succinctly tells of God's extraordinary love. He loves you and everyone in the world so much that He gave up His only Son, Jesus, to die on the cross to pay the price for the sin of every person. And then Jesus rose to life again, showing how He conquers death and gives forever life to those who humble themselves, repent of sin, and believe in Him as Savior. There is no greater hope!

Heavenly Father, thank You for the love and hope You have given me and all people because You sent Jesus to die to save the world from the punishment of sin. Thank You that He rose to life again and that I have forever life too, because I believe in Him as my one and only Savior. Help me to share the good news of Your great love! Amen.

Kept in the Love of God

But you, beloved, building yourselves up in your most holy faith and praying in the Holy Spirit, keep yourselves in the love of God, waiting for the mercy of our Lord Jesus Christ that leads to eternal life.

JUDE 1:20-21 ESV

How do you keep yourself in the love of God? Do you spend time learning from Him? Do you regularly read His Word? Do you talk to God through prayer and have quiet time to listen for answers? Do you go to a Bible-teaching church to worship and learn? Do you serve Jesus by serving others? Do you have other strong Christians in your life who help remind you of and encourage you in God's truth and love? Do you fill your mind with songs of praise to Him? Through His Holy Spirit, God is with you always, but sometimes it's easy to ignore His presence. We have to be diligent and intentional to keep ourselves in His love.

Heavenly Father, I want to keep myself in Your love, staying in close relationship with You! Please help me to never forget or ignore You. Amen.

He Commands Even Winds and Water

*One day he got into a boat with his disciples, and he said
to them, "Let us go across to the other side of the lake."
So they set out, and as they sailed he fell asleep. And a
windstorm came down on the lake, and they were filling
with water and were in danger. And they went and woke
him, saying, "Master, Master, we are perishing!" And
he awoke and rebuked the wind and the raging waves,
and they ceased, and there was a calm. He said to them,
"Where is your faith?" And they were afraid, and they
marveled, saying to one another, "Who then is this, that he
commands even winds and water, and they obey him?"*

LUKE 8:22–25 ESV

Jesus can command anything in all of creation to obey Him.
He could simply speak words to a storm to make it stop. He
has extraordinary, supernatural power over everything, and
He's your Savior who loves and cares for you. Remembering
these truths can fill you with great hope and courage to face
any hard thing.

---

*Dear Jesus, You can speak the words to stop the storm
in my life. But even if you don't right now, You will
eventually in Your perfect timing. Most importantly,
I know You won't leave me in the midst of the storm.
I put my trust and hope in You alone. Amen.*

Imagine the Best, Not the Worst

God is our safe place and our strength. He is always our help when we are in trouble. So we will not be afraid, even if the earth is shaken and the mountains fall into the center of the sea, and even if its waters go wild with storm and the mountains shake with its action.

PSALM 46:1–3 NLV

Sometimes we feel hopeless and full of fear because we imagine the worst that can happen and then focus on that. So we need this scripture to remind us that there is no horrible thing we can think of that God cannot deliver us from. He is always our help when we are in trouble, no matter how awful the situation. Instead of imagining the worst, we should focus on the best—the truth that God is our safe place and our strength!

Heavenly Father, I trust that You protect and save from even the worst kind of trouble. Thank You that You will always be my hope and my help. Amen.

Share Your Gifts

God has given each of you a gift from his great variety
of spiritual gifts. Use them well to serve one another.
Do you have the gift of speaking? Then speak as
though God himself were speaking through you. Do
you have the gift of helping others? Do it with all the
strength and energy that God supplies. Then everything
you do will bring glory to God through Jesus Christ.
All glory and power to him forever and ever!

1 PETER 4:10-11 NLT

God has given you special gifts, but they are not for you
alone. Don't ever just keep them to yourself. Share your
gifts with others—those talents and abilities and skills that
come easily to you. God has given them to you so you can
serve and encourage and bless others. If you don't already
know, pray and ask God to help you recognize the things
you're especially good at and exactly how He wants you to
use those abilities. Most of all, constantly thank God and give
credit to Him for every wonderful thing you can do. Every
good thing is a gift from Him.

Heavenly Father, thank You for the talents and abilities
You have given me. Help me to know how best to use
them to share Your hope and love. I want to worship
You and bless and encourage others. Amen.

Healing from Past Sin

The LORD is merciful and gracious, slow to anger and abounding in steadfast love. He will not always chide, nor will he keep his anger forever. He does not deal with us according to our sins, nor repay us according to our iniquities. For as high as the heavens are above the earth, so great is his steadfast love toward those who fear him; as far as the east is from the west, so far does he remove our transgressions from us.

PSALM 103:8-12 ESV

Our enemy Satan doesn't want us to heal from our past sins. He wants us to agonize over them endlessly, beat ourselves up, and live in dejection and defeat so that we feel far away from God. But the truth is that when we repent of our sins, God takes them as far away from us as possible—as far as the east is from the west—so that we can draw as close to Him as possible. He is merciful and gracious and loving. He wants to completely heal our hearts and minds from the sins of our past so that we live in spiritual and mental wellness and victory, ready and able to do every good thing He has planned for us.

Heavenly Father, please help me never to agonize over past sin I have repented of. I know You have completely removed it from me. I can't ever thank You enough. Your mercy, grace, and love are far greater than I deserve, and I am grateful! Amen.

Cleansed

*Don't you realize that those who do wrong will not
inherit the Kingdom of God? Don't fool yourselves.
Those who indulge in sexual sin, or who worship idols,
or commit adultery, or are male prostitutes, or practice
homosexuality, or are thieves, or greedy people, or
drunkards, or are abusive, or cheat people—none of these
will inherit the Kingdom of God. Some of you were once
like that. But you were cleansed; you were made holy;
you were made right with God by calling on the name
of the Lord Jesus Christ and by the Spirit of our God.*

1 CORINTHIANS 6:9-11 NLT

So much hope and healing can be found in the amazing grace
Jesus offers to anyone who believes in Him. Any sin can be
cleansed by the blood of Jesus' sacrifice of Himself on the
cross for the sins of all people. " 'Come now, let's settle this,'
says the LORD. 'Though your sins are like scarlet, I will make
them as white as snow. Though they are red like crimson, I
will make them as white as wool'" (Isaiah 1:18 NLT).

*Dear Jesus, thank You that anyone can call on You
to be cleansed and saved from sin because You
sacrificed Yourself on the cross to pay the penalty.
Please keep calling me and all people everywhere
to sincere repentance and steadfast hope in You.*

You Are Weak; God Is Not

Christ is not weak when He works in your hearts. He uses His power in you. Christ's weak human body died on a cross. It is by God's power that Christ lives today. We are weak. We are as He was. But we will be alive with Christ through the power God has for us.

2 CORINTHIANS 13:3–4 NLV

When you're feeling weak, don't feel hopeless, and don't beat yourself up. The truth is that you *are* weak as a human being in your human body. But God is not weak. Remember that with the Holy Spirit in you, you have the same power working in you that raised Jesus from death to life. That's incredible! Whatever God has planned for you to do, you can trust that you will be able to do it well. He will give you the gifts and strengths and tools you need to do it. And someday God's power in you will enable you to live forever in heaven too!

Heavenly Father, thank You that You are never weak. You are my strength. You are my power. You are my hope. Amen.

No Matter the Past

Jesus said to her, "Mary." She turned and said to him in Aramaic, "Rabboni!" (which means Teacher). Jesus said to her, "Do not cling to me, for I have not yet ascended to the Father; but go to my brothers and say to them, 'I am ascending to my Father and your Father, to my God and your God.'" Mary Magdalene went and announced to the disciples, "I have seen the Lord"—and that he had said these things to her.

JOHN 20:16-18 ESV

Mary Magdalene had a terrible life before she met Jesus. After He cast seven demons out of her (Luke 8:2), she was beyond grateful and became a close follower. When Jesus was crucified, Mary Magdalene was there and must have been devastated. But then she was also there when Jesus rose from the dead, and we can only imagine the joy she must have felt! She was the very first to see Jesus again after He had come back to life. Mary Magdalene's story offers tremendous hope to anyone who has experienced a terrible life before coming to trust in Jesus. He has the power to completely transform, renew, and bless anyone's life, no matter their past.

Heavenly Father, help me to remember that no one is hopeless. You have the power to rescue anyone from any terrible situation and then transform and renew and bless them incredibly. Amen.

Darkness into Light

And I will lead the blind in a way that they do not know, in paths that they have not known I will guide them. I will turn the darkness before them into light, the rough places into level ground. These are the things I do, and I do not forsake them.

ISAIAH 42:16 ESV

When we're facing big problems or have big choices to make, sometimes we feel totally blind, like we just can't see the right way to go or the best thing to do. So the promises and hope God gives in this scripture are soothing and refreshing. We can trust that He will turn the darkness into light and make the rough places smooth for His people. He will open up new paths for us when we don't know what to do or where to go. He never leaves us to face anything alone, and He never breaks a promise.

Heavenly Father, I'm hoping and trusting in You because I know You keep Your promises. And You have promised to guide Your people well. Please guide me right now. Show me Your will and Your way for my life. Amen.

The Lord Will Watch over You

I will lift up my eyes to the mountains. Where will my help come from? My help comes from the Lord, Who made heaven and earth. He will not let your feet go out from under you. He Who watches over you will not sleep. Listen, He Who watches over Israel will not close his eyes or sleep. The Lord watches over you. The Lord is your safe cover at your right hand. The sun will not hurt you during the day and the moon will not hurt you during the night. The Lord will keep you from all that is sinful. He will watch over your soul. The Lord will watch over your coming and going, now and forever.

PSALM 121 NLV

No one cares for you or watches over you as well as God does. He does not get tired; He never needs to sleep. Every time you need a fresh dose of hope and help, look up to remember that He is Creator of the mountains and the heavens and the earth—and don't forget that He is within you through His Spirit too.

Heavenly Father, You are my constant hope and helper and hero. Thank You for always watching over me, now and forever. Amen.

When the Battle Is God's

"Listen, all you people of Judah and Jerusalem! Listen, King Jehoshaphat! This is what the LORD says: Do not be afraid! Don't be discouraged by this mighty army, for the battle is not yours, but God's. . . . You will not even need to fight. Take your positions; then stand still and watch the LORD's victory. He is with you, O people of Judah and Jerusalem. Do not be afraid or discouraged. Go out against them tomorrow, for the LORD is with you!"
2 CHRONICLES 20:15–17 NLT

When a problem in your life seems too overwhelming for you to handle, take heart by thinking of this story of King Jehoshaphat in the Bible. God told His people who were up against a great enemy army that the battle was not theirs but His. He told them they wouldn't even need to fight but should just stand and watch His saving power work for them. Sometimes all you need to do is just stand strong in your faith and watch what God does to rescue you from trouble.

Heavenly Father, please show me when I just need to take my position, stand still, and then watch Your victory in the battle going on in my life. I trust You to fight for me! Amen.

Lessons from Tabitha

There was a believer in Joppa named Tabitha.... She was always doing kind things for others and helping the poor.

ACTS 9:36 NLT

Tabitha was known for being good and kind and making lovely clothing for others. When she became sick and died, two of her friends went to Peter to beg for his help. Her friends knew Peter had been a disciple of Jesus who had the power to heal in His name. Peter agreed and went to the house where they had laid her body. Her friends were gathered around her, crying. Peter told them all to leave the room, and then he knelt down and prayed. Afterward, he said to Tabitha, "Get up," and she opened her eyes and sat up! By the power of Jesus, Peter had healed Tabitha so that she came back to life! Very likely she then went right back to doing the many good and kind things she loved to do.

Heavenly Father, thank You for the example of Tabitha to inspire me to be generous and to use the talents You've given me to love and encourage others. And thank You for healing her through the power You gave to Peter to show that You are the God of hope and miracles! Amen.

On Level Ground

Teach me to do your will, for you are my God;
may your good Spirit lead me on level ground.
For your name's sake, LORD, preserve my life;
in your righteousness, bring me out of trouble.
PSALM 143:10-11 NIV

Are you letting God lead you on level ground? How does that show in your life—at home and work and church? In your relationships? In your activities and hobbies? Keep asking God to lead you every day. Let Him guide you out of trouble if you're in it, and let Him steer you away from trouble. Let Him give you the best kind of life because you want to be taught by Him and seek to do His will.

Heavenly Father, I want Your good Spirit inside me
to lead me on level ground. Help me to stay out of
trouble and follow You no matter what, knowing
that You are always right and good. Amen.

Don't Worry; Pray Instead

Do not be anxious about anything, but in every situation, by prayer and petition, with thanksgiving, present your requests to God. And the peace of God, which transcends all understanding, will guard your hearts and your minds in Christ Jesus.

PHILIPPIANS 4:6–7 NIV

Worry will only make you weak, but prayer packs a powerful punch. When you pray and ask God for what you need, remember to focus on what you've already been given. As you think of the many ways God has already blessed you and provided for you, you'll find yourself wondering, *What is there to worry about? Nothing!* Just like He has in the past, God will continue to bless you and provide for you. Thank Him and praise Him for who He is and all He has done. Then let His amazing peace fill you up so much that there's no room for whatever worries you might have.

Heavenly Father, I don't want to be weak with worry. Help me to remember the tremendous power in prayer! Thank You for all the ways You have blessed me and helped me and for all the ways You will continue to do so. Amen.

Yet There Is Hope

I am sure that our suffering now cannot be compared to the shining-greatness that He is going to give us. Everything that has been made in the world is waiting for the day when God will make His sons known. Everything that has been made in the world is weak. It is not that the world wanted it to be that way. God allowed it to be that way. Yet there is hope. Everything that has been made in the world will be set free from the power that can destroy.

ROMANS 8:18–21 NLV

Often when we're begging God for help and an answer to our prayers, He doesn't just suddenly fix things the way we want. We really wish He would—so when He doesn't, our hope in Him can be shaken as we wonder why. In times like these, we must seek wisdom in His Word—from passages like Romans 8—and praise God for the ways He is answering our prayer in others ways, even when we don't see the exact answer we'd like. And we must keep trusting, keep hoping, keep standing strong in faith.

Heavenly Father, please help me to keep trusting You even when I'm feeling confused and discouraged about why You don't answer the way I want You to. Please hold me when I'm hurting and guide me with wisdom from Your Word. Amen.

Consumed by Anguish

*Be merciful to me, LORD, for I am in distress; my
eyes grow weak with sorrow, my soul and body
with grief. My life is consumed by anguish and
my years by groaning; my strength fails because
of my affliction, and my bones grow weak.*

PSALM 31:9-10 NIV

Can you relate to the agony in this passage? The book of
Psalms includes many instances of wrestling with emotion.
These passages are timelessly understandable. Psalms also
contains images of great comfort and peace. Notice that after
more lament, David, the writer of this psalm, turns to praise
and hope again, saying, "But I trust in you, LORD; I say, 'You
are my God.' My times are in your hands" (Psalm 31:14-15 NIV).

*Dear Lord, like David, I do feel like my life is consumed by
anguish right now. But still I trust in You. I know You are
sovereign. You are my one true God, and every moment
of my life is in Your hands. Fill me with peace despite
my pain, and show me Your will day by day. Amen.*

Power over Every Kind of Evil

Once when we were going to the place of prayer, we were met by a female slave who had a spirit by which she predicted the future. She earned a great deal of money for her owners by fortune-telling. She followed Paul and the rest of us, shouting, "These men are servants of the Most High God, who are telling you the way to be saved." She kept this up for many days. Finally Paul became so annoyed that he turned around and said to the spirit, "In the name of Jesus Christ I command you to come out of her!" At that moment the spirit left her.

ACTS 16:16–18 NIV

This poor girl was demon-possessed and a slave to the men making money off of her as she predicted the future. When she met Paul, the demon inside her made her follow Paul and his friends to mock them. But because of the power of Jesus working through Paul, he was able to command the demon to come out of the girl and stop controlling her. Even now, thousands of years later, slavery, demon possession, and mockery of Christians are still happening in our world. But praise God that Jesus has power over every kind of evil, and our hope is in Him to conquer it all!

Dear Jesus, thank You for Your power to rescue people from every evil thing. I pray that You would keep working Your power to rescue people who need it every day. Please show me how I can help! Amen.

Nothing Can Keep Us from the Love of God

Who can keep us away from the love of Christ? Can trouble or problems? Can suffering wrong from others or having no food? Can it be because of no clothes or because of danger or war? The Holy Writings say, "Because of belonging to Jesus, we are in danger of being killed all day long. We are thought of as sheep that are ready to be killed." But we have power over all these things through Jesus Who loves us so much. For I know that nothing can keep us from the love of God. Death cannot! Life cannot! Angels cannot! Leaders cannot! Any other power cannot! Hard things now or in the future cannot! The world above or the world below cannot! Any other living thing cannot keep us away from the love of God which is ours through Christ Jesus our Lord.

ROMANS 8:35–39 NLV

Sometimes we feel hopeless because of catastrophic thinking. But even the worst thing we imagine going wrong can never keep God's love away from us. He will never stop caring for you. Let that truth fill you with hope this very moment and every moment here on out.

Heavenly Father, remind me every moment that nothing can keep me away from Your love. You have saved me through Jesus. I am cared for and protected and full of great hope because I am Yours! Amen.

Patient Perseverance

Be patient, then, brothers and sisters, until the Lord's coming. See how the farmer waits for the land to yield its valuable crop, patiently waiting for the autumn and spring rains. You too, be patient and stand firm, because the Lord's coming is near. Don't grumble against one another, brothers and sisters, or you will be judged. The Judge is standing at the door! Brothers and sisters, as an example of patience in the face of suffering, take the prophets who spoke in the name of the Lord. As you know, we count as blessed those who have persevered. You have heard of Job's perseverance and have seen what the Lord finally brought about. The Lord is full of compassion and mercy.

JAMES 5:7-11 NIV

Just as a farmer has to persevere patiently through all sorts of trials and uncertainties to bring in a valuable crop, we who follow Jesus must also persevere patiently in life as the Lord works in this world to bring people to saving faith in Him. Our attitudes and actions and willingness to be used by God in the midst of hardship can either help or hinder the spreading of His truth and love through the Gospel.

Heavenly Father, help me to stand firm and patiently persevere in all things. I know You are doing good work gathering people into Your kingdom through Your Son, Jesus Christ. Please use me in that wonderful work! Amen.

An Everlasting Crown

Do you not know that in a race all the runners run, but only one gets the prize? Run in such a way as to get the prize. Everyone who competes in the games goes into strict training. They do it to get a crown that will not last, but we do it to get a crown that will last forever.

1 CORINTHIANS 9:24-25 NIV

How we run our race here on earth, on the path God has mapped out for us, matters—*a lot!* And it's no regular race. It's a race with eternal significance, to win a forever crown. So we should do our very best to live God-honoring lives—to use the gifts God has given us to serve Him and others, to do the good things He has planned for us, and to help others love Jesus and give God all the glory!

Heavenly Father, help me not to forget that every day I'm running an important race You've put me in here on earth. Please help me to run well, looking ahead to a perfect prize in heaven—a crown that will last forever. Amen.

Hope from the Past

Then Moses said to the people, "Remember this day in which you came out from Egypt, out of the house of slavery, for by a strong hand the LORD brought you out from this place."

EXODUS 13:3 ESV

Sometimes we just want to forget hardship and loss and pain because they were awful and we're so glad they're in the past. Yet in some ways, remembering them can give us great hope. We must never forget how God helped us through them or rescued us from them. Looking back and remembering grows our faith and trust that God will help and rescue again in the future. Moses told the people of Israel to remember the amazing day that God finally brought them out of slavery in Egypt. Just as they did, we too need to remember the times God has rescued us from trials and tribulations.

Heavenly Father, every bit of help and rescue I have ever received has ultimately come from You! I don't want to forget! Build my faith and hope in You as I recall even the hardest things in the past and remember how You carried me through. Amen.

God Sent His Angel

The king declared to Daniel, "O Daniel, servant of the living God, has your God, whom you serve continually, been able to deliver you from the lions?" Then Daniel said to the king, "O king, live forever! My God sent his angel and shut the lions' mouths, and they have not harmed me, because I was found blameless before him."
DANIEL 6:20-22 ESV

God could have made Daniel fly out of the den. He could have killed the lions. He could have made the king switch places with Daniel. He could have saved Daniel in any way He chose. But God sent His angel to shut the mouths of the lions. God can send his angels to help and rescue you too—at any moment and for any reason—in ways you may never even realize.

Heavenly Father, You have angels You can send to help me anywhere, anytime. Remembering Your host of angels gives me hope and courage to face any problem or challenge or danger or fear that might come my way. Amen.

Sit at the Lord's Feet

A woman named Martha welcomed [Jesus] into her house. And she had a sister called Mary, who sat at the Lord's feet and listened to his teaching.

LUKE 10:38-39 ESV

When you're feeling hopelessly unproductive, as if you never quite get enough accomplished, remember the story of Mary and Martha. They were two sisters who were excited to welcome Jesus into their home. Martha excelled at hosting and tending to all the details of good hospitality. But Martha grew very frustrated with Mary because when Jesus arrived, Mary didn't help her with all those detailed tasks. Mary simply sat at Jesus' feet to listen to everything He had to say. Both sisters loved Jesus and were showing it in their own ways. But Jesus lovingly told Martha that Mary had chosen what was best, urging her not to fuss so much over the work to be done but to simply enjoy His company and listen to His teaching.

Dear Jesus, I want to show my love to You by the good works I can do, like Martha; but I also want to choose the best way by enjoying simply being with You, like Mary. Please help me to choose what is best. Amen.

Extraordinary Endurance

We have this treasure in jars of clay to show that this all-surpassing power is from God and not from us. We are hard pressed on every side, but not crushed; perplexed, but not in despair; persecuted, but not abandoned; struck down, but not destroyed.

2 CORINTHIANS 4:7-9 NIV

In what ways are you feeling hard pressed on every side today? Perplexed? Persecuted? Struck down? You might feel like you can't bear another second of the hardship you are going through, but trust this scripture. No matter what's happening, you will *not* be crushed. You will *not* fall into despair. You will *never* be abandoned. You will *never* be destroyed. God will help you have extraordinary endurance. He will give you just enough fresh strength and energy and hope and joy at just the right moments. Hang in there with faith and confidence in the one true almighty God! You can trust His Word and His promises.

Heavenly Father, when I feel like I'm at my breaking point, remind me You'll never let that happen. You are sovereign and good! You give me supernatural strength, endurance, hope, and joy!

They Feared God

*The king of Egypt said to the Hebrew midwives,
whose names were Shiphrah and Puah, "When you
are helping the Hebrew women during childbirth on
the delivery stool, if you see that the baby is a boy,
kill him; but if it is a girl, let her live." The midwives,
however, feared God and did not do what the king of
Egypt had told them to do; they let the boys live.*

EXODUS 1:15-17 NIV

The Hebrew midwives were told to kill the Hebrew baby
boys, but they would not do it. Why? Because they "feared
God." They respected Him and knew He was greater than
any earthly power. They trusted that if they did the right
thing—refusing to kill innocent babies—God would protect
and bless them. And they were exactly right. Scripture goes
on to say, "God was kind to the midwives and the people
increased and became even more numerous. And because
the midwives feared God, he gave them families of their
own" (Exodus 1:20-21 NIV).

*Almighty God, I respect and trust and hope in You
far more than any earthly power or authority. Help
me to always do what is right in Your eyes. Amen.*

Courage and Cleverness

When she could hide him no longer, she got a papyrus basket for him and coated it with tar and pitch. Then she placed the child in it and put it among the reeds along the bank of the Nile. His sister stood at a distance to see what would happen to him.

EXODUS 2:3–4 NIV

One of the Israelite babies saved from Pharaoh's evil plan was Moses, and his mother was Jochebed. When it became too difficult to keep hiding and protecting baby Moses as he grew, Jochebed showed courage and clever thinking. She came up with a plan to put Moses in a basket in the river near where Pharaoh's daughter liked to bathe. Jochebed hoped the princess would find Moses and adopt him as her own. And that's exactly what happened. Moses was safe and could grow up to be the great leader God planned for him to be!

Heavenly Father, please help me to have hope and courage like Jochebed. Give me clever ideas when I need them to help carry our Your perfect plans. Amen.

Until the Very Last Moments

*One of the criminals who were hanged railed at him,
saying, "Are you not the Christ? Save yourself and us!"
But the other rebuked him, saying, "Do you not fear God,
since you are under the same sentence of condemnation?
And we indeed justly, for we are receiving the due
reward of our deeds; but this man has done nothing
wrong." And he said, "Jesus, remember me when you
come into your kingdom." And he said to him, "Truly, I
say to you, today you will be with me in paradise."*

LUKE 23:39–43 ESV

Jesus gives grace until even the very last moments of life,
wanting everyone to believe in Him and receive Him as
Savior. If you have friends and loved ones who are not yet
believers, keep on hoping for them, praying for them, and
sharing God's great love with them. Jesus wants to give them
every chance possible for eternal life in paradise.

*Dear Jesus, thank You for the example of the criminal
beside You who believed at the last moment. It gives me
so much hope for people I know who don't yet trust in You.
Please humble them and soften their hearts to You! Amen.*

The Spirit Intercedes

Likewise the Spirit helps us in our weakness. For we do not know what to pray for as we ought, but the Spirit himself intercedes for us with groanings too deep for words. And he who searches hearts knows what is the mind of the Spirit, because the Spirit intercedes for the saints according to the will of God.

ROMANS 8:26–27 ESV

Sometimes you might feel so hopeless, so scared and worried, that you don't have the slightest clue how to pray. That's when you must remember you have the Holy Spirit in you who actually prays for you when you can't find the words. Incredible! Thank God for that blessing, and let it fill you with hope and courage. God never leaves you. He always knows everything you think and everything you need. He helps you even when you don't know how to ask for help!

Heavenly Father, thank You for Your Holy Spirit who acts as my helper and even prays for me when I don't know how. Thank You for knowing me better than I know myself! Amen.

God Turns Mourning into Dancing

"Hear me, LORD, and have mercy on me. Help me, O LORD."
You have turned my mourning into joyful dancing. You
have taken away my clothes of mourning and clothed
me with joy, that I might sing praises to you and not be
silent. O LORD my God, I will give you thanks forever!

PSALM 30:10-12 NLT

Only our awesome, loving God can take any kind of grief, anxiety, sorrow, or pain in our lives and turn it into such joy that we feel like dancing. He might do that for us here on earth in certain ways, or we might have to wait until heaven—but we can trust that He will. With every hard thing you might go through, you have a choice to either pull away from God or to cling more tightly to Him. The first choice will only bring despair, but the second choice will lead to dancing!

Heavenly Father, I want to get closer to You in the midst
of hardship and pain. I trust that You will turn every
sorrow into complete joy and dancing someday. Amen.

God of the Weather

"God's voice is glorious in the thunder. We can't even imagine the greatness of his power. He directs the snow to fall on the earth and tells the rain to pour down. Then everyone stops working so they can watch his power."

JOB 37:5-7 NLT

Scientists today can make all kinds of smart predictions about the weather and climate change, but no one can control it except the One who created it—our extraordinary God! Let the weather fill you with greater awe and respect for Him. Bow before Him in humility and ask for His protection, provision, and care. Thank Him when the weather blesses you, and choose to trust and praise Him even when it doesn't—because you know you are a child of the powerful King who commands it, who uses it any way He chooses to work out His perfect plans.

Heavenly Father, my hope is not in this world or in any brilliant person who makes predictions or plans here. No one is sovereign like You are! You are awesome and mighty and in control of all things. Amen.

Jesus Is the Resurrection and the Life

Jesus called in a loud voice, "Lazarus,
come out!" The dead man came out.

JOHN 11:43-44 NIV

As shown in the miraculous account of the resurrection of Lazarus from the dead, Jesus had all power to heal and raise the dead to life and still does today—according to His will and to help people believe in Him—through the Holy Spirit. But when He doesn't choose to heal in this life, don't forget Martha's and Jesus' exchange from earlier in this same passage of scripture:

"Lord," Martha said to Jesus, "if you had been here, my brother would not have died. But I know that even now God will give you whatever you ask."

Jesus said to her, "Your brother will rise again."

Martha answered, "I know he will rise again in the resurrection at the last day."

Jesus said to her, "I am the resurrection and the life. The one who believes in me will live, even though they die; and whoever lives by believing in me will never die. Do you believe this?" (John 11:21-26 NIV).

Heavenly Father, I trust Your ability to heal and raise the dead to life. I know You have power to do so at any time, in any place; and ultimately I believe with all my heart that You raise to eternal life everyone who believes in You as Savior. Amen.

Because of His Greatness

It is God Who sits on the throne above the earth. The people living on the earth are like grasshoppers. He spreads out the heavens like a curtain.... It is He Who brings rulers down to nothing. He makes the judges of the earth as nothing.... Lift up your eyes and see. Who has made these stars? It is the One Who leads them out by number. He calls them all by name. Because of the greatness of His strength, and because He is strong in power, not one of them is missing.
ISAIAH 40:22-23, 26 NLV

How does being compared to just a grasshopper give us any hope? Because it reminds us of God's awesome greatness. He spread out the skies as easily as if they were curtains. He is able to defeat any human power or scheme. He made the stars and counts them and even has a name for each of them. And this same amazing God knows and cares about every single detail of each one of us too! We are so small compared to God, yet we are dearly loved and perfectly cared for by His almighty hand.

Heavenly Father, You fill me with such hope and courage because I know You are so much bigger than me and anything in this world—and You are always taking care of me. Thank You! Amen.

Hope in a Difficult Workplace

Whatever you do, work at it with all your heart, as working for the Lord, not for human masters, since you know that you will receive an inheritance from the Lord as a reward. It is the Lord Christ you are serving.
COLOSSIANS 3:23–24 NIV

In a hopeless-seeming work situation, let God help you find joy and purpose in the work anyway. What is your attitude like at work? How could it change if you applied this scripture from Colossians to it? (Look up and apply Philippians 2:13–15 to your attitude too!) No matter what kind of work situation you're in, picture God as your boss overseeing you. He's your heavenly Father and the very best leader. He loves you more than anyone ever, and He blesses and rewards good work like no one else can. So do all your work with all your heart! Let God teach you and grow you and give you joy through everything—even when it feels hard and hopeless. He will either change your attitude or change your situation as you trust Him to guide you and care for you.

Heavenly Father, please help me with my work when it feels hopeless and unbearable. Please either change my attitude so I can have joy or change my work situation. Either way, I trust that You never stop helping me and loving me. I want to do all things for Your glory! Amen.

New Every Morning

But this I call to mind, and therefore I have hope: The steadfast love of the LORD never ceases; his mercies never come to an end; they are new every morning; great is your faithfulness. "The LORD is my portion," says my soul, "therefore I will hope in him."

LAMENTATIONS 3:21–24 ESV

As you wake up to a new day, hopefully you've had a good night's rest and feel like you have a fresh start, no matter what happened yesterday. God's Word talks about how God's love and mercy are new to us every morning. On good mornings and on those not-so-good mornings, as you open your eyes and climb out of bed, reflect on this scripture and let it give you courage and hope for whatever you're facing that day.

Heavenly Father, thank You for brand-new days that offer a fresh start. I hope in You and Your great faithfulness, love, and mercy today! Amen.

He Will Not Stop Helping You

David said to his son Solomon, "Be strong. Have strength of heart, and do it. Do not be afraid or troubled, for the Lord God, my God, is with you. He will not stop helping you. He will not leave you until all the work of the house of the Lord is finished."

1 CHRONICLES 28:20 NLV

When you're facing a challenge or a lot of hard work that feels overwhelming and stirs up fear and anxiety, sometimes you just need a little pep talk like Solomon got from his dad. Do you have people in your life who give you good pep talks? Thank them for their encouragement; and thank God for blessing you with their presence in your life. Other times you just need to remember scriptures like this and let God's Word give you the exact pep talk you need, like "Be strong and brave, and just do it! Don't be afraid, because God is with you! He won't stop helping you; He will never leave you!"

Heavenly Father, thank You for the people who give me good pep talks and also for all the pep talks that come from Your Word! Help me to remember them exactly when I need them. Amen.

Hope in the Good Shepherd

"I am the good shepherd. The good shepherd lays down his life for the sheep. The hired hand is not the shepherd and does not own the sheep. So when he sees the wolf coming, he abandons the sheep and runs away. Then the wolf attacks the flock and scatters it. The man runs away because he is a hired hand and cares nothing for the sheep. I am the good shepherd; I know my sheep and my sheep know me—just as the Father knows me and I know the Father—and I lay down my life for the sheep."

JOHN 10:11-15 NIV

Jesus said He is the Good Shepherd, and then later He proved it by giving up His own life to save others from sin. Anyone who trusts in Jesus as Savior becomes a sheep under Jesus' care—and that's a wonderful creature to be, a wonderful place to be. Think of the specific ways you have seen His care and guidance, and trust that He will never stop loving and shepherding you.

Dear Jesus, thank You for letting me be Your sheep. I want to be guided and cared for by You forever! Amen.

Confidently Trust the Lord

How joyful are those who fear the LORD and delight in obeying his commands. Their children will be successful everywhere; an entire generation of godly people will be blessed. They themselves will be wealthy, and their good deeds will last forever. Light shines in the darkness for the godly. They are generous, compassionate, and righteous. Good comes to those who lend money generously and conduct their business fairly. Such people will not be overcome by evil. Those who are righteous will be long remembered. They do not fear bad news; they confidently trust the LORD to care for them.

PSALM 112:1-7 NLT

Those of us who fear the Lord have such great hope for both this life and the life to come. God wants to bless us both now and eternally for loving and following Him.

Heavenly Father, thank You for the promises in this psalm. I confidently trust that You care for me and want to bless me in amazing ways as I put all my hope in You! Amen.

A Broken Promise

*Peter replied, "Even if all fall away on account of
you, I never will." "Truly I tell you," Jesus answered,
"this very night, before the rooster crows, you will
disown me three times." But Peter declared, "Even if
I have to die with you, I will never disown you."*

MATTHEW 26:33-35 NIV

Have you ever broken a promise and felt helpless to regain
trust and mend the relationship? There is hope even then.
Remember, for example, Peter's big broken promise to Jesus. He had told Jesus that there was no way he would ever
deny knowing Him. It was unthinkable to Peter. But then
when Jesus was captured and taken to be killed, Peter did
deny Jesus, just like Jesus had warned. Afterward, Peter felt
awful and bitterly ashamed of himself (Matthew 26:69-75).
Still, Jesus loved and forgave Peter, and Peter went on to do
great things to spread the news of Jesus. Jesus loves and
forgives us and never wants to hold our sins against us when
we confess and repent.

*Dear Jesus, help me to remember that even though
Peter messed up big-time, there was still hope. There's
hope for me too when I break promises and make
mistakes. Remind me how You love to forgive. Amen.*

Hope in the Best Boss

If your sinful old self is the boss over your mind, it leads to death. But if the Holy Spirit is the boss over your mind, it leads to life and peace. The mind that thinks only of ways to please the sinful old self is fighting against God. It is not able to obey God's Laws. It never can. Those who do what their sinful old selves want to do cannot please God. But you are not doing what your sinful old selves want you to do. You are doing what the Holy Spirit tells you to do, if you have God's Spirit living in you.

ROMANS 8:6-9 NLV

Before we trust in Jesus as Savior, our sin nature tells us what to do. And if we let sin be our boss, we are hopeless—we will regularly choose selfishness and greed. We will mostly be looking out for ourselves, and in the end we will destroy ourselves. But once we trust Jesus, we have His Holy Spirit living inside us, and He is the very best boss who always wants the very best for us. He will lead us in a life of loving God and loving others and being filled with joy as we share the Good News and spread hope for eternal life.

Heavenly Father, thank You for saving me and taking me from being a hopeless slave to sin and making me a hopeful follower of the very best boss—Your Holy Spirit. Help me to choose to obey You every day! Amen.

Not Ashamed

I am not ashamed of the gospel, because it is the power of God that brings salvation to everyone who believes.

ROMANS 1:16 NIV

Despite what the world might tell us, we have no reason to ever feel embarrassed or ashamed of believing in Jesus. Like Paul in the Bible, we should want to be able to say this—that we are not ashamed of the good news that Jesus came to earth to live a perfect life and teach us, died on the cross to pay for our sins, then rose to life again and offers us eternal life too. When we share this good news and awesome hope with others, we help spread God's power to save people from their sins.

Heavenly Father, help me to never feel ashamed or embarrassed to share the good news about Jesus! Thank You for the true hope You give and for wanting to save all people from their sins! Amen.

Even If

The Lord is my light and the One Who saves me. Whom should I fear? The Lord is the strength of my life. Of whom should I be afraid? When sinful men, and all who hated me, came against me to destroy my flesh, they tripped and fell. Even if an army gathers against me, my heart will not be afraid. Even if war rises against me, I will be sure of You.

PSALM 27:1–3 NLV

Let this scripture give you strength and courage and inspire you to think of all kinds of "even if" statements to proclaim the hope God gives you, like these:

- "Even if the diagnosis isn't good, I trust You to take care of me and my family, God!"

- "Even if I don't get this job, I will trust You to provide for me, God!"

- "Even if this hardship doesn't go away, I know You will guide me as I endure it, God!"

- "Even if I make mistakes, I know You love and forgive me, God!"

Heavenly Father, thank You that no matter what uncertainties I face in life, I can be totally sure of You! Even if everything else falls apart, You never do; and I never will when I'm holding on to You. Amen.

Praise the Creator

O LORD, what a variety of things you have made! In wisdom you have made them all. The earth is full of your creatures.
PSALM 104:24 NLT

Whenever you get to spend time outside, whenever you do anything that makes you focus on and appreciate the natural world around you, remember to give praise to our Creator God! He has designed all of creation with incredible love and purpose. Every extraordinary detail of it reminds us in countless ways how awesome He is. The God who planned and created land and sky and sea and plants and animals certainly has great plans for men and women who are created in His image. Keep hoping in Him, seeking Him, and asking Him to show you His great plans for you.

Heavenly Father, just looking around outside fills me with great hope because Your creation is so meticulously designed and beautiful. I trust that You created me with beautiful plans too. Please show them to me in Your perfect timing. Amen.

Just Abide

"Already you are clean because of the word that I have spoken to you. Abide in me, and I in you. As the branch cannot bear fruit by itself, unless it abides in the vine, neither can you, unless you abide in me. I am the vine; you are the branches. Whoever abides in me and I in him, he it is that bears much fruit, for apart from me you can do nothing."

JOHN 15:3-5 ESV

Jesus described Himself as a vine and God the Father as the gardener. We are the branches. The fruit we grow on our branches consists of the good things we do for God that He has planned for us—like serving and caring for others, sharing God's love, and helping others to know Jesus as Savior. At times we may become discouraged, feeling as if we aren't producing enough good fruit. But Jesus says simply to abide in Him—and as a result of that relationship, we will produce plenty, according to His will. We don't have to worry and wonder about the size of the crop; we simply focus on loving our Savior and staying close to Him, getting life from Him. Then He will make the fruit grow.

Dear Jesus, my life is from You and for You.
I want to abide in close relationship with You.
Keep me close and grow in me the good fruit
You want to produce through my life! Amen.

Waiting for the Lord

I did not give up waiting for the Lord. And He turned to me and heard my cry. He brought me up out of the hole of danger, out of the mud and clay. He set my feet on a rock, making my feet sure. He put a new song in my mouth, a song of praise to our God. Many will see and fear and will put their trust in the Lord.

PSALM 40:1-3 NLV

It's hard to be patient while we wait with hope. But even when it seems like it's taking God forever to answer your prayers, don't give up. At just the right time, He will answer and help you according to His will. And like this psalm says, He will bring you out of danger and onto solid rock. Then you'll be singing new songs to God, and many will see what happened and hear your praise and put their trust in God too! Remember that your patient, steadfast faith sets an example for others to hope in God as well.

Heavenly Father, I want to have patient, steadfast faith. I never want to give up on waiting for You. Please help me to keep hanging on, waiting with joyful hope for Your perfect timing and plans. Amen.

Proving Your Faith and Sharing Hope

There is wonderful joy ahead, even though you must endure many trials for a little while. These trials will show that your faith is genuine. It is being tested as fire tests and purifies gold—though your faith is far more precious than mere gold. So when your faith remains strong through many trials, it will bring you much praise and glory and honor on the day when Jesus Christ is revealed to the whole world.

1 PETER 1:6-7 NLT

When we keep our faith in Jesus as our Savior through all kinds of pain and hardship, we prove our faith is real and set an example of hope for others. Saying we love and trust Jesus during good times is easy, but saying we love and trust Him even when we go through bad times is not. Your faith is the most valuable thing about you, worth so much more than gold or any kind of treasure. So keep asking God to grow and strengthen it, and don't be surprised that it will be tested sometimes. Hold on to God during those testing times and see how your faith develops an extraordinary new shine that helps light the way for others.

Heavenly Father, please help me to pass the tests of my faith well. I want to keep holding on to You—proving that my faith is genuine and sharing my hope in You with others! Amen.

When Your Heart Is Sad

*Why am I discouraged? Why is my heart so
sad? I will put my hope in God! I will praise
him again—my Savior and my God!*

PSALM 42:11 NLT

When we put our hope in anything other than God, we will
always end up discouraged and sad. We might find temporary encouragement and happiness, but it won't last. First
John 2:17 (NLT) says, "This world is fading away, along with
everything that people crave. But anyone who does what
pleases God will live forever." And that forever life that God
guarantees is our motivation and a source of real hope and
real encouragement. It's the reason we can have true and
lasting deep-down joy, not just fickle, fleeting happiness.

*My Savior and my God, I put all my hope in You, and I
praise You! Remind me that when I'm feeling discouraged
and sad, it's because my attention is not on You and the
forever life You promise. When my heart is downcast and
heavy, please lighten it and lift it back to You. Amen.*

God's Hand

*Even if I walk into trouble, You will keep my life
safe. You will put out Your hand against the anger
of those who hate me. And Your right hand will
save me. The Lord will finish the work He started for
me. O Lord, Your loving-kindness lasts forever.*
PSALM 138:7-8 NLV

Is there anyone in your life who truly seems to hate you?
Anyone purposefully trying to put you in danger or make
your life miserable? Do you feel like the situation will never
get better? If that's the case, remember and pray this scripture. God will keep your life safe in any kind of trouble. He
can put out His hand to protect you against any danger or
malice from anyone who might treat you hatefully. Pray to
ask Him to do so, and thank and praise Him when He does!

*Heavenly Father, I feel hated by some people right
now, and I'm overwhelmed. Please put out Your
hand against them to protect and save me. I trust
in Your everlasting love and kindness. Amen.*

Don't Neglect Meeting Together

Let us hold tightly without wavering to the hope we affirm, for God can be trusted to keep his promise. Let us think of ways to motivate one another to acts of love and good works. And let us not neglect our meeting together, as some people do, but encourage one another, especially now that the day of his return is drawing near.

HEBREWS 10:23–25 NLT

In a world full of sadness and pain, sin and temptation, and Satan's lies and schemes, we Christians must intentionally and firmly keep our grip on our hope in Jesus Christ. We must constantly remind each other of it and encourage each other in it. That's why being part of a true, whole-Bible-teaching church is so important. We need regular fellowship and support so we can encourage each other to never let go of hope and motivate each other in acts of love and good works that will spread our faith in Jesus to others, so they might trust in Him too.

Heavenly Father, I trust Your promises and want to hold tightly to my hope in You through Your Son, Jesus Christ. Help me to have fellowship with other believers that encourages and motivates both me and them and also spreads hope to others around us. Amen.

Your Safe Place

My soul is quiet and waits for God alone. My hope comes from Him. He alone is my rock and the One Who saves me. He is my strong place. I will not be shaken. My being safe and my honor rest with God. My safe place is in God, the rock of my strength. Trust in Him at all times, O people. Pour out your heart before Him. God is a safe place for us.

PSALM 62:5-8 NLV

When you think of your safe place, do you think of the place you feel most comfortable and relaxed and understood? Maybe you think of being at home with your family, cozy and secure. Or maybe you think of being with your best friend—the person you can talk to about anything. Those are wonderful safe places, but God wants to be your very best, strongest, most secure safe place! He is with you anytime and anywhere. Talk to Him, cry out to Him, depend on Him, and trust Him for everything you need.

Heavenly Father, You are my solid rock and safe place everywhere I go and in every situation I encounter. Thank You that I can pour out my heart to You anytime, anywhere. Amen.

Little Girl, Get Up!

*When they came to the home of the synagogue leader,
Jesus saw much commotion and weeping and wailing.
He went inside and asked, "Why all this commotion
and weeping? The child isn't dead; she's only asleep."
The crowd laughed at him. But he made them all
leave, and he took the girl's father and mother and
his three disciples into the room where the girl was
lying. Holding her hand, he said to her, "Talitha koum,"
which means "Little girl, get up!" And the girl, who was
twelve years old, immediately stood up and walked
around! They were overwhelmed and totally amazed.*

MARK 5:38-42 NLT

We don't know what illness Jairus's daughter had that made
her so sick that she died, but we can tell that she was dearly
loved by her dad and mom and many others. Her dad had
great faith that Jesus could come and simply put His hand on
her and she would live. And he was right. Jesus went home
with Jairus to the room were his daughter lay. Jesus took her
by the hand, and with just one short command—"Little girl,
get up!"—she was healthy and whole!

*Heavenly Father, You are the amazing God of
life and miracles! Thank You for the awesome
ways Jesus has showed us Your love and
power to heal and give life. Amen.*

You Can Always Be Sure of God

The Lord is my light and the One Who saves me. Whom should I fear? The Lord is the strength of my life. Of whom should I be afraid? When sinful men, and all who hated me, came against me to destroy my flesh, they tripped and fell. Even if an army gathers against me, my heart will not be afraid. Even if war rises against me, I will be sure of You.

PSALM 27:1–3 NLV

Let this psalm give you strength and confidence and hope! With the Lord as your light and as the One who saves you, nothing and no one should ever make you feel afraid. There's not a lot in this world you can be sure of these days, but you can always be absolutely sure of Him—sure of His power and protection and provision for you, and especially sure of His great love for you!

Heavenly Father, thank You that I can be totally, completely, 100 percent sure of You! Amen.

Remember God's Red Sea Miracle

Moses stretched out his hand over the sea, and the
LORD drove the sea back by a strong east wind all
night and made the sea dry land, and the waters
were divided. And the people of Israel went into the
midst of the sea on dry ground, the waters being a
wall to them on their right hand and on their left.

EXODUS 14:21–22 ESV

What an awesome miracle—God's parting of the Red Sea to
rescue His people from the Egyptians pursuing them. What
an astounding sight that must have been! Walls of water on
the left and right and dry ground to walk on in the midst
of the sea? Just unreal! And the same God who parted the
waters is the One who sees and knows and loves you right
now. He is awesome beyond your wildest imagination, and
He is able to make a way through whatever Red Sea kind of
problem or pain you need to cross right now. Praise Him for
His greatness and goodness and power. Keep hoping and
trusting in Him!

Heavenly Father, You are amazing beyond description.
I trust that You can do absolutely anything to rescue
Your people, including me! All my hope is in You! Amen.

A Future and a Hope

" 'For I know the plans I have for you,' says the Lord, 'plans
for well-being and not for trouble, to give you a future
and a hope. Then you will call upon Me and come and
pray to Me, and I will listen to you. You will look for Me
and find Me, when you look for Me with all your heart.' "
JEREMIAH 29:11-13 NLV

Let these words spoken through the prophet Jeremiah to
the people of Israel encourage you as you ask God to show
you His specific plans for your future. Look back and thank
Him for how He has guided you in the past to provide for
you and bless you. Acknowledge and repent of those times
when you went your own way instead of following His lead.
And remember that no matter what twists and turns life takes
here on earth, the best future and hope that God is planning
for you is forever in heaven.

Dear Lord, I call upon You! Please lead me in the good
plans You have for me. Help me not to go my own way.
Help me to look for You with all my heart. Amen.

Hope in Suffering

In his kindness God called you to share in his eternal glory by means of Christ Jesus. So after you have suffered a little while, he will restore, support, and strengthen you, and he will place you on a firm foundation. All power to him forever! Amen.

1 PETER 5:10-11 NLT

Suffering in our earthly life is inevitable but not endless. As this scripture promises, after you've experienced suffering, God will restore you, support you, strengthen you, and place you on a firm foundation once again. Let this promise give you hope in the midst of your trial and pain today. It will not last forever. Keep moving forward; keep holding tightly to faith in our Savior. In His perfect timing, He will rescue you from it; and in the midst of it, He will never leave you.

Heavenly Father, I know You have all power to rescue me from this suffering in my life and I trust You will at exactly the right time. Show me Your presence and encouragement in the midst of it. Amen.

All the Days of Your Life

*O Lord, you alone are my hope. I've trusted you,
O LORD, from childhood. Yes, you have been with me
from birth; from my mother's womb you have cared
for me. No wonder I am always praising you!*

PSALM 71:5-6 NLT

Think of all the people throughout your life, from the time
you were born until now, whom God has provided to care
for you and bond with you. Praise Him for all those people
and for His love! Ultimately God is the One who constantly
watches over you, and He works through many different
people to care for you. He always has and always will. Believe this promise from Psalm 23:6 (ESV): "Surely goodness
and mercy shall follow me all the days of my life, and I shall
dwell in the house of the LORD forever."

*Dear Lord, thank You for the people You have placed
in my life, some for just a season and some for the long
haul, who care for me and connect with me with love that
ultimately comes from You! I trust that Your goodness
and mercy follow me daily and that You will always
provide me with the people I need in my life. Amen.*

You Belong to the Lord!

Be full of joy always because you belong to the Lord.
Again I say, be full of joy! Let all people see how
gentle you are. The Lord is coming again soon.
PHILIPPIANS 4:4–5 NLV

Be full of joy always? *Ha! Not possible*, you might be thinking. What's joyful about a broken relationship or a loved one dying? What's joyful about the loss of a job or a home? What's joyful about experiencing abuse or neglect, addiction or illness? It's true, those things certainly are not joyful. But you can still be full of supernatural joy in the midst of them because of one important truth: if you trust Jesus as your Savior, you belong to the Lord! All of those unjoyful things that happen here on earth are just temporary, but the perfect home God is creating for us in heaven lasts forever. Jesus is coming again soon, and we will live there forever with Him—with no suffering ever again!

Dear Lord, remind me every moment that I belong to
You! That's where my supernatural true joy comes from,
even in the midst of any kind of hardship. Amen.

Ask for Good Glimpses

*"No eye has seen, no ear has heard, and no mind
has imagined what God has prepared for those
who love him." But it was to us that God revealed
these things by his Spirit. For his Spirit searches out
everything and shows us God's deep secrets.*

1 CORINTHIANS 2:9-10 NLT

What do you dream and hope for the future? And what do you imagine about heaven? As you dream and imagine, remember 1 Corinthians 2:9-10. We can never fully imagine all the good and awesome things God has planned for us because our human brains just aren't capable! But if we stay strong in our faith in God, we can ask the Holy Spirit within us to show us good glimpses! What good glimpses are you seeing from God these days?

*Heavenly Father, I trust You have amazing plans
and blessings for me both here on earth and forever
in heaven. Show me glimpses, please! Amen.*

Hope in the Alpha and Omega

"I am the First and the Last. I am the beginning and the end."

REVELATION 22:13 NLV

Jesus says several times in the Bible that He is the first and the last, the beginning and the end. Some Bible translations use the words Alpha and Omega; those are the names of the first and last letters in the Greek alphabet. He is A and Z in our alphabet. Jesus is everything, and He has always existed. He has gone before us, and He goes ahead of us. He surrounds us on all sides. We struggle to wrap our minds around this truth, but we can rest in the fact that Jesus knows and always has known the whole story of our lives.

Dear Jesus, You are the beginning and the end of all things. I am so blessed to call You my hope and my Savior. Amen.

They Who Wait upon the Lord

Have you not known? Have you not heard? The God Who lives forever is the Lord, the One Who made the ends of the earth. He will not become weak or tired. His understanding is too great for us to begin to know. He gives strength to the weak. And He gives power to him who has little strength. Even very young men get tired and become weak and strong young men trip and fall. But they who wait upon the Lord will get new strength. They will rise up with wings like eagles. They will run and not get tired. They will walk and not become weak.

ISAIAH 40:28–31 NLV

Imagine never feeling weak or tired! What would you do with all that extra energy and time? With so many activities and stressors in life, our minds just can't fully comprehend it. But our Creator God has endless strength and power. He never falters, and He never fails to share His strength and power with us exactly when we need it. He renews, refreshes, and rejuvenates us time and again—not always according to our preferred schedule, but always according to His perfect timeline.

Heavenly Father, fill me with new strength and power when I'm weak and tired. I trust that You can and You will in Your perfect timing. I wait with great hope in You! Amen.

One True Religion

*We need such a Religious Leader Who made the way
for man to go to God. Jesus is holy and has no guilt. . . .
Christ is not like other religious leaders. They had to give
gifts every day on the altar in worship for their own sins
first and then for the sins of the people. Christ did not
have to do that. He gave one gift on the altar and that gift
was Himself. It was done once and it was for all time.*

HEBREWS 7:26-27 NLV

Plenty of people might say that all religions are the same, but
it's just not true. Our only real hope is belief in Jesus as God
and Savior. Jesus alone was perfect and holy and without
sin. He is the one and only Way, Truth, and Life (John 14:6).
He died as a sacrifice for sin for all people of all time, and
He rose to life again with eyewitness proof. No other religion
offers that kind of gift and love and miracle! To know Jesus as
Savior is simply to believe in Him and accept His awesome
gift of grace and eternal life. He gave this gift when He died
on the cross, taking our sins away, and then rose to life again.

*Dear Jesus, no one else is like You! You are
God and You are Savior, and all my hope is
in You! I am so grateful for You! Amen.*

Sharing Hope with Future Generations

I remember your genuine faith, for you share the faith that
first filled your grandmother Lois and your mother, Eunice.
And I know that same faith continues strong in you.

2 TIMOTHY 1:5 NLT

The Bible doesn't say much about two women named Lois and Eunice, but what it does say can inspire us to greater hope for future generations and motivate us to set wonderful examples of faith for them. These two women were the grandmother and mother to a young Christian named Timothy. His friend was Paul, who wrote many of the letters in the New Testament of the Bible. The book of 2 Timothy is one of Paul's letters to Timothy to encourage him in his faith. Paul reminds Timothy of the true faith of his grandma and mom, Lois and Eunice. What an honor for these ladies to be remembered this way! Think about how you would like your faith to be remembered. Be strong and keep growing in it so that others will say your faith was always genuine, and they will be inspired likewise.

Heavenly Father, I want to be known for
having true faith in You that I share with future
generations, just like Lois and Eunice. Amen.

The Hope to Which He Has Called You

I keep asking that the God of our Lord Jesus Christ,
the glorious Father, may give you the Spirit of wisdom
and revelation, so that you may know him better. I pray
that the eyes of your heart may be enlightened in order
that you may know the hope to which he has called
you, the riches of his glorious inheritance in his holy
people, and his incomparably great power for us who
believe. That power is the same as the mighty strength
he exerted when he raised Christ from the dead and
seated him at his right hand in the heavenly realms.

EPHESIANS 1:17-20 NIV

This prayer of the apostle Paul for the Christians who lived
in Ephesus is what God wants for you as a Christian today
too. If you believe in Jesus as your only Savior, you belong
to Him and you have hope for the awesome things God has
planned for you. What's more, His power—the same power
that brought Jesus back to life—is working in you now to help
you do the good things God wants for you. That awesome
power will be working in you forever, because it has given
you eternal life!

Heavenly Father, every day please help me to see and
know how awesome You are and how awesome
Your plans and Your power in my life are. Increase
my faith and hope more and more. Amen.

Never Give Up

One day Jesus told his disciples a story to show that they should always pray and never give up. "There was a judge in a certain city," he said, "who neither feared God nor cared about people. A widow of that city came to him repeatedly, saying, 'Give me justice in this dispute with my enemy.' The judge ignored her for a while, but finally he said to himself, 'I don't fear God or care about people, but this woman is driving me crazy. I'm going to see that she gets justice, because she is wearing me out with her constant requests!' " Then the Lord said, "Learn a lesson from this unjust judge. Even he rendered a just decision in the end. So don't you think God will surely give justice to his chosen people who cry out to him day and night? Will he keep putting them off? I tell you, he will grant justice to them quickly!"

LUKE 18:1–8 NLT

This parable from Jesus reminds us never to give up hope in our prayers. He urges us to be persistent in prayer. We can cry out to Him constantly, day and night, and trust that He will answer.

Dear Jesus, thank You for this story assuring me You never want me to give up hope when I'm praying to You! I will keep on asking for Your help in all things. Amen.

A Place Prepared for You

"Let not your hearts be troubled. Believe in God; believe also in me. In my Father's house are many rooms. If it were not so, would I have told you that I go to prepare a place for you? And if I go and prepare a place for you, I will come again and will take you to myself, that where I am you may be also. And you know the way to where I am going."

JOHN 14:1-4 ESV

Jesus is preparing a home for us in heaven, but like Thomas, sometimes we might wonder if we know exactly how to get there (John 14:5 ESV). Jesus answered him, "I am the way, and the truth, and the life. No one comes to the Father except through me" (John 14:6 ESV). And so we get there by following Jesus throughout this earthly life until one day we are in forever life in the home He has prepared for us in heaven. How do we follow Him? By reading His Word, living our lives humbly surrendered to His will, and trusting we are guided by the Holy Spirit.

Dear Jesus, remind me every moment that You are the one and only Way, Truth, and Life through this world. I will keep following You until the day I come home to be with You in perfect paradise forever. I'm so excited for that day! Amen.

The Lord Stands with You

*The first time I was brought before the judge, no one
came with me. Everyone abandoned me. May it not
be counted against them. But the Lord stood with
me and gave me strength so that I might preach the
Good News in its entirety for all the Gentiles to hear.
And he rescued me from certain death. Yes, and
the Lord will deliver me from every evil attack and
will bring me safely into his heavenly Kingdom.*

2 TIMOTHY 4:16-18 NLT

Have you experienced, like Paul in this scripture, a time
when everyone you knew abandoned you? Yet Paul didn't
want to hold it against his friends, because even with no one
else there to help, God Himself was with Paul and protected
him and gave him power. How have you seen God help you
like that? Paul trusted that God would keep away every evil
plan that anyone might have against him. Do you trust that
too? Paul also knew that someday God would bring him
into heaven forever. And God promises that for you as well!

*Heavenly Father, I trust that no matter what happens
here in this world, ultimately You will always keep
me safe because someday You are going to bring me
into perfect paradise in heaven with You! Amen.*

No Need to Worry

*"Therefore I tell you, do not be anxious about your life,
what you will eat or what you will drink, nor about your
body, what you will put on. Is not life more than food,
and the body more than clothing? Look at the birds of
the air: they neither sow nor reap nor gather into barns,
and yet your heavenly Father feeds them. Are you not
of more value than they? And which of you by being
anxious can add a single hour to his span of life?"*

MATTHEW 6:25-27 ESV

When you trust God, you will always have what you need.
He is your perfect provider! If you're ever fretting about
finances or work or food or clothes or anything at all, come
again to this scripture in Matthew 6. Read and believe that
God takes good care of even the birds of the air—surely He
takes even better care of you!

*Heavenly Father, I don't want to be anxious about
anything. Please take these worries of life from
me. Remind me how You always provide for my
every need. I hope and trust in You. Amen.*

Watch the Sky

*A cloud carried Him away so they could not see Him.
They were still looking up to heaven, watching Him
go. All at once two men dressed in white stood beside
them. They said, "You men of the country of Galilee,
why do you stand looking up into heaven? This same
Jesus Who was taken from you into heaven will return
in the same way you saw Him go up into heaven."*
ACTS 1:9–11 NLV

After Jesus died and rose again, He remained on earth for
forty days to prove Himself alive and teach His followers some
more before going up to heaven in a cloud. His friends kept
watching the sky, but then two angels appeared and said,
"What are you doing? He'll come back again someday." It
was time for His followers to get busy sharing about Jesus.
Do you ever wish Jesus would hurry back and appear in the
sky again? It will be amazing! But while we wait, we need
to keep busy sharing the hope of the good news that Jesus
died to save us from our sin and that He is alive now and will
take all who trust in Him to heaven someday!

*Dear Jesus, I'm watching the sky for You, but I'll
also keep busy sharing Your Good News! Amen.*

Hope in the Real Deal

Our God is in the heavens. He does whatever He wants to do. Their gods are silver and gold, the work of human hands. They have mouths but they cannot speak. They have eyes but they cannot see. They have ears but they cannot hear. They have noses but they cannot smell. They have hands but they cannot feel. They have feet but they cannot walk. They cannot make a sound come out of their mouths. Those who make them and trust them will be like them.

PSALM 115:3-8 NLV

This psalm compares our one true God with the fake gods of the world that some people make for themselves. It describes how ridiculous those fake gods are—they have useless mouths, eyes, ears, noses, hands, and feet. But people often make fake gods, because they don't really want to serve or worship anyone but themselves. And so they will end up as useless and meaningless as those fake gods. But to trust and obey and worship our extraordinary God, who is the real deal, is to live the life you were created for, with love and hope and peace forever.

One true God, I'm so thankful I hope and trust in You, not a fake god. Help me to keep living for You and sharing You with others. Amen.

How Much Can We Give?

Command those who are rich in this present world not to be arrogant nor to put their hope in wealth, which is so uncertain, but to put their hope in God, who richly provides us with everything for our enjoyment. Command them to do good, to be rich in good deeds, and to be generous and willing to share. In this way they will lay up treasure for themselves as a firm foundation for the coming age, so that they may take hold of the life that is truly life.

1 TIMOTHY 6:17-19 NIV

Our hopes and goals here on earth should never be about how much we can get. Rather, they should be about how much we can give, how many good works we can do to encourage others for God's glory, and to point others to salvation in Jesus Christ. We are called to be generous givers with our money and with our blessings, which ultimately come from God. His Word tells us to be ready to share and give and help others in need—and promises that we will gather up forever treasure in heaven by doing so. Money and the blessings of this world are only temporary, but the good and giving kinds of things we have done here on earth will matter in heaven for all eternity.

Heavenly Father, help me to make goals based on how much I can give, not how much I can get. I hope and trust in Your promises about blessings and treasures in heaven. Amen.

Our Blessed Hope

For the grace of God has appeared, bringing salvation for all people, training us to renounce ungodliness and worldly passions, and to live self-controlled, upright, and godly lives in the present age, waiting for our blessed hope, the appearing of the glory of our great God and Savior Jesus Christ, who gave himself for us to redeem us from all lawlessness and to purify for himself a people for his own possession who are zealous for good works.

TITUS 2:11-14 ESV

Our blessed hope is the appearing of Jesus. We are always to be watching for His return. He promises He will, and it will be unlike anything any person has ever experienced. It will be wonderful for everyone who loves and trusts in Him as Savior. Mark 13:24-27 (NLT) says: "At that time, after the anguish of those days, the sun will be darkened, the moon will give no light, the stars will fall from the sky, and the powers in the heavens will be shaken. Then everyone will see the Son of Man coming on the clouds with great power and glory. And he will send out his angels to gather his chosen ones from all over the world—from the farthest ends of the earth and heaven."

Dear Jesus, You are my blessed hope! I'm watching and waiting for You to return and gather Your people, including me! I love You and trust You! Amen.

Fix Your Eyes on Jesus

Therefore, since we are surrounded by such a great cloud of witnesses, let us throw off everything that hinders and the sin that so easily entangles. And let us run with perseverance the race marked out for us, fixing our eyes on Jesus, the pioneer and perfecter of faith. For the joy set before him he endured the cross, scorning its shame, and sat down at the right hand of the throne of God. Consider him who endured such opposition from sinners, so that you will not grow weary and lose heart.

HEBREWS 12:1-3 NIV

Sometimes we allow things into our lives that drain us and hinder us and make us lose focus on the great hope we have in Jesus. Can you take time to evaluate what's weighing you down and especially repent of any sin you are holding on to? Like the psalmist, pray, "Create in me a pure heart, O God, and renew a steadfast spirit within me" (Psalm 51:10 NIV). Then fix your eyes on Jesus and keep running with perseverance the race God has set for you, doing all the good things He has planned for you along the way.

Dear Lord, please help me to rid my life of anything that takes my focus off of You. My life is in You and for You, and I want to run well this race You have set for me, until I'm with You at the finish line. Amen.

Hope for Our Dream Home

*How beautiful are the places where You live, O Lord of all!
My soul wants and even becomes weak from wanting to
be in the house of the Lord.... How happy are those who
live in Your house! They are always giving thanks to You.*

PSALM 84:1-2, 4 NLV

Do you ever think about and hope for a dream house? What
would it look like, and where would it be located? It's fun to
imagine! But better than any home we can dream up here on
earth is the forever home God is creating for us in heaven.
And when we take time to focus on God and praise Him and
hear from Him through His Word, we get little glimpses of
how incredible that perfect forever home will be!

*Heavenly Father, thank You for my blessings here
and now where I live on earth; but even more,
thank You for the perfect home with You that You
are making in heaven for me forever! Amen.*

A Living Body That Lasts Forever

*Our body is like a house we live in here on earth. When it
is destroyed, we know that God has another body for us in
heaven.... This body will last forever. Right now we cry inside
ourselves because we wish we could have our new body
which we will have in heaven. We will not be without a body.
We will live in a new body. While we are in this body, we cry
inside ourselves because things are hard for us. It is not that
we want to die. Instead, we want to live in our new bodies. We
want this dying body to be changed into a living body that
lasts forever. It is God Who has made us ready for this change.
He has given us His Spirit to show us what He has for us.*

2 CORINTHIANS 5:1-5 NLV

There's no stopping the aging process, no hope for immortality
in these earthly bodies. But we have certain and secure hope,
because of Jesus, that God is preparing new bodies for us in
heaven that will be forever young. And while at times, we do
cry inside ourselves as we experience the brokenness of this
world, we always have the Holy Spirit within us to encourage
us and remind us of God's promises and truth.

*Heavenly Father, I'm eager for my heavenly body
and home that will last forever, but I'm also grateful
for each day You give me on this earth. Help me
to do all the good things You have planned for
me—until one day I become the new flawless me
at home forever with You in heaven. Amen.*

Trustworthy and True

Then I saw "a new heaven and a new earth," for the first heaven and the first earth had passed away, and there was no longer any sea. I saw the Holy City, the new Jerusalem, coming down out of heaven from God, prepared as a bride beautifully dressed for her husband. And I heard a loud voice from the throne saying, "Look! God's dwelling place is now among the people, and he will dwell with them. They will be his people, and God himself will be with them and be their God. 'He will wipe every tear from their eyes. There will be no more death' or mourning or crying or pain, for the old order of things has passed away." He who was seated on the throne said, "I am making everything new!" Then he said, "Write this down, for these words are trustworthy and true."

REVELATION 21:1-5 NIV

These words from Jesus are not just an empty or uncertain hope. They are solid and sure, "trustworthy and true." They are the ultimate, guaranteed reward of those who humbly put their trust in Jesus Christ as their one and only Savior from sin. Our perfect dwelling place with God, with no more sorrow or pain, is not *if* but *when*. Hallelujah!

Jesus my Savior, I expectantly, eagerly await that wonderful day when You make all things new. Until then, help me to live my life loving and serving You. Amen.

Scripture Index

OLD TESTAMENT